PRACTICAL HAPPINESS

A YOUNG MAN'S GUIDE TO A CONTENTED LIFE

BOB SCHULTZ

GREAT EXPECTATIONS BOOK CO.

Eugene, Oregon 97402

Scripture quotations are taken from the King James Version of the Bible.

Practical Happiness: A Young Man's Guide to a Contented Life
Copyright ©2008 Bob Schultz
All rights reserved

Illustrated by Emily Schultz
Cover Design by Alpha Advertising
Interior Design by Pine Hill Graphics

Publisher's Cataloging-in-Publication Data
(Provided by Cassidy Cataloguing Services, Inc.)

Schultz, Bob.

    Practical happiness : a young man's guide to a contented life / Bob
Schultz. -- 1st ed. -- Eugene, Ore. : Great Expectations Book Co.,
2008.

    p. ; cm.
    ISBN: 978-1-883934-13-2
    Includes bibliographical references.

    1. Happiness--Religious aspects--Christianity. 2. Attitude
(Psychology) 3. Young men--Spritual life. I. Title.

BF575.H27 S38 2008
248.832--dc22   0802

Printed in the United States of America.

13 14 15 16 17 18 19 20 / 15 14 13 12 11 10 9 8 7 6 5

Dedicated to Molly, Emily, and Betsy

Introduction

For six years my family and I lived in a travel trailer. During that time we bought some wooded acreage, cleared a site, milled lumber, and built a house. It took a lot of work and left little time for play. My youngest daughter worked beside me whenever she could. My oldest, though not inclined toward construction, frequently sat nearby chatting or simply watching the progress. I began to notice that my middle daughter wasn't coming out much anymore. When I asked why, she said, "I don't like being around people who aren't happy, and you're not happy."

If someone had asked, "Are you happy?" I would have said, "Of course!" I had a great job, a super family, land to work, health, friends, a Christian perspective, and yet…her words were true; I was missing something.

Since that day, over fifteen years ago, I've taken a serious look at what makes a man happy and have recorded the highlights here. This book is an attempt to equip young men with a few tools to help them overcome the selfishness and discouragement that rob a man of the joy God offers. These are the things I wish someone had told me when I was a boy.

Bob Schultz

Contents

Chapter 1

Questions

He that questioneth much, shall learn much.

—Francis Bacon

Throughout my life I've enjoyed being the kid. When I was just beginning my career as a carpenter I liked my role as the youngest on the framing crew. Being the kid meant there was always someone nearby who had more experience, knowledge, and understanding to answer my questions and solve my problems. People don't mind *much* when a kid asks lots of questions.

In many areas of life, I still see myself as the kid. When trouble arises with my car or pickup, I head across the street to my neighbor's house. "Bill, the paint on my truck has lost its shine. What can I do about it?" Bill's been working on cars longer than I've been alive. In his garage is a 1941 Ford delivery van, jet black except for the yellow flames on the front fenders. It's all I can do to keep from running my hand over its smooth shining metal. A gorgeous car!

"I think I've got something over here, somewhere," Bill drawls as he rummages through a bench covered with bottles and cans of oil, car wash, transmission fluid, WD-40, windshield-washing soap, rear-end grease, carburetor cleaner, spray paint, gasket sealer, and a lot of other stuff I don't recognize. "Here it is," he announces as he pulls up a half used bottle of some specialty compound. "This'll do ya."

With the highest respect for a man who knows how to put a shine on a car, I thank him and head home. Besides carrying the rubbing compound, I carry that kid feeling: I don't know anything compared to him.

It's too bad that everybody who owns a car can't have a neighbor like Bill. Whatever he gave me worked. In a few hours the hood of my 77 Ford pickup looked almost like new.

In nearly every area of life, there's somebody to look up to. Whenever I get the chance I like to ask these men what they've seen, that I might understand more of how life works.

I'm just finishing a carpentry job for a man named Tom. His life fascinates me. I would like to visit with him for hours, asking questions about his work, what he did in his family that turned out well, what didn't. I'd like to hear about his childhood, his schooling, and how he chose his career. Maybe he would tell me more about what it's like to land a jet on an aircraft carrier at night, in a storm, with an all but empty fuel tank. He's only a year or two older than me, yet I feel like a youngster beside him and eagerly welcome any opportunity to see life through his eyes.

As fellow workers retire and friends die, I'm realizing that in some areas of life I'm no longer the kid. I look over my shoulder and see many younger guys behind me who haven't had my experiences, nor seen what I've seen. They don't have gray hair, a wrinkled face, nor do they need reading glasses.

I never want to lose the kid feeling and the hunger to learn from the wise around me. I'd still rather sit beside Grandpa Dow asking him questions and hearing his perspective on life, yet it's time for me to offer my experiences to those younger who want to know them.

On November 18, 1967, I began reading my Bible daily and applying its lessons to everyday situations. I've come to learn by experience that the God who created the world and used about forty men over the course of some fifteen hundred years to write the Bible is the same God who controls life's events today. He's knowable, trustworthy, and kind. It's because of these experiences with Him that I write what I've seen.

I wish we could meet in my office and have a face to face talk; however, it's only a four-by-eight room off my woodshop. After crowding in a desk, computer, filing cabinet, and bookshelves, there's only room for one folding chair for any guests. Better yet I'd enjoy gathering around the woodstove, sitting on a five-gallon bucket or leaning against the table saw. Again, that's just not practical, for most of you don't live anywhere near Walterville.

The next best thing is for me to come into my office alone, open the door to the warmth of the shop and, as personally as possible, write about how God has expressed Himself through everyday life to me. That's what I'm attempting to do.

In the past, I've already written to some of you about general things boys face in the book *Boyhood and Beyond*. After that I've given you *Created for Work*, stories specifically for young men about seeing God while taking their first steps in the business world. Why am I writing to you about practical happiness now?

To answer that question I have to go back twenty years to the day my wife said to me, " I'd rather live in a garage that's paid for than a house that's not." That statement started us on an adventure that drastically altered our lives. We asked the question, "Could a family live in America during the twenty-first century without borrowing money for anything?" We began that day to see if it was possible. We sacrificed many comforts, worked long hours, and made our share of mistakes along the way. Times were often tough as I worked my regular carpentry job during the day and diligently labored building our own home every spare moment. My youngest daughter worked by my side, learning her fractions from a measuring tape and developing a mind for hard work. My oldest daughter's interests were in keeping house, not carpentry. Nevertheless, she would often come out and sit nearby, keeping us entertained with friendly chatter. I began to notice I rarely saw my middle daughter.

One day I asked her, "Emily, you don't come around much any more while we're working. Why is that?" Without pausing to think about it she answered, "I don't like being around people that aren't happy; and you're not happy."

Her words hit me like the time the backhoe operator accidentally dropped the bucket on my head. Me, not happy? If someone had asked I would have answered, "Of course I'm happy!" I had a super family, a great job, land to work, health, friends, a Christian perspective, and yet…her words were true, I was missing something.

For fifteen years I've taken a serious look at what makes a man happy. The highlights of my discoveries appear in the following chapters. This isn't a comprehensive discussion of happiness. It's simply some things I've discovered while eagerly looking for the answers to my questions from everyone I met and especially from the One to whom I'll always be a kid, my Father in Heaven. It's my attempt to pass on to men, young and old, a few tools that have helped me overcome some of the selfishness and discouragement that had robbed my joy, through good times and assorted trials. These are lessons I wish some older man had told me when I was young.

Though you're in various stages of manhood, may these stories encourage you to seek God for yourself, like an inquisitive child, with all your heart, mind, soul and strength.

> *But Jesus called them unto him, and said, Suffer [allow] little children to come unto me, and forbid them not: for of such is the kingdom of God. Verily I say unto you, Whosoever shall not receive the kingdom of God as a little child shall in no wise enter therein.* (Luke 18:16-17)

Questions

- What is a one-word question that little children ask many times each day?

- How does asking questions express humility?

- Why don't proud people like to ask questions?

- In the context of this chapter, at what age does a man stop feeling like a kid?

- What was the question my wife and I asked that drastically changed our family's life?

Chapter 2

Deep-Sea Diving

This is a noble magnificence of thought, a true religious greatness of mind, to be thus affected with God's general providence, admiring and magnifying His wisdom in all things; never murmuring at the course of the world, or the state of things, but looking upon all around, at heaven and earth, as a pleased spectator, and adoring that invisible Hand, which gives laws to all motions, and overrules all events to ends suitable to the highest wisdom and goodness.

—William Law

My friend Ralph believes God created the earth. He explores as much of it as possible because it helps him to grasp the greatness and beauty of his Creator. He has traveled over most of the U.S., including a cruise to Alaska, visited Africa for a couple of safaris, been to Australia, China and toured in the Middle East. Each year he plans a number of trips that expose him and his family to God's handiwork. Though he may enjoy restaurants and museums, his attention focuses upon the land, the waterways, the animals, and the plants; he wants to see the glory of God.

It's fascinating to hear Ralph's enthusiasm and excitement as he describes the places he's discovered. One evening, he told me about underwater diving adventures. He says there's a wonderland living under the waves few men ever experience. With camera in hand, he has enjoyed plunging into the ocean and slowly descending toward the bottom. As fellow divers kicked swiftly here and there attempting to view it all, Ralph floated upright, as if standing in a bus. His usual style was to place one hand under his camera, bracing it to his chest, and the other behind his back to avoid any foolish moves. Then Ralph submitted himself to the current, and drifted wherever it took him.

When his diving friends created their own currents by strong arm strokes or powerful finned kicks, the delicate creatures on the ocean floor sensed their approach and hid themselves from these strange intruders. On the contrary, as Ralph quietly floated by, they confidently opened and blossomed. As a result they offered him a gorgeous show of beauty.

One particular creature was the Christmas tree worm. When free from fear they seemed to grow out of the rocks like a four-inch forest of fir trees, decked out in a rainbow of colors. Any unfamiliar currents send them instantly into holes and crevices. But, as Ralph rested in the current, they posed for his camera, unaware that he recorded their beauty for land lovers like me.

Nature responds the same whether underwater or on a wilderness mountain slope. A loud brush-crashing hiker may catch a fleeting glimpse of some animal; however, he'll never watch a cow elk nurse her calf or a wolverine sun himself upon a rock.

Young boys have a tendency to run through the woods using a stick as an imaginary sword, stabbing and slashing at everything in sight, never seeing the amazing plants and animals all around them. It requires a measure of maturity before they begin to think of anything outside of themselves. Once a young man enters the woods with an eye to see its beauty and quietly waits and watches, nature rewards him with fascinating experiences, giving him an understanding that there's more to life than himself.

Wisdom responds just like nature. The old proverb says, "Blessed [or happy] is the man that heareth me, watching daily at my gates, waiting at the posts of my doors. For whoso findeth me findeth life, and shall obtain favor of the Lord."[1]

---

1. Proverbs 8:34-35

When a man walks quietly through life, flowing with its pace, looking and listening, the whole world opens to him. A quick trip to the gas station may become a lesson in compassion if you watch the attendant patiently help a disoriented traveler instead of spending your time fiddling with the CD player.

By quietly asking questions with a sincere interest in a person, you'll often discover a beautiful or fascinating heart. If you approached the same individual with the selfishness of running through the woods and whacking everything with a stick, you would hardly even know they existed. People don't open their hearts to preoccupied, fast-paced individuals; they will to those who make the time to sit quietly, ask gently, and listen intently.

I'm not talking about lazing around doing nothing. I'm describing tiptoeing through life, spotting and recording the secret wonders of existence. It's attentively floating along, watching people, their relationships, and characteristics. It's observing actions and their related consequences. It might be watching animals with an eye for beauty and learning lessons from their God-given instincts. All of life opens before the young man who will drift through it like Ralph, capturing pictures of sea worms.

Suppose it's your turn to clean out the chicken house. One method is to sprint to the pen, dash through the yard into the coop sending the terrified flock flapping and stampeding into the wire fencing; with a whirlwind of energy shovel the floor, change the water, restraw the nesting boxes, hang up a new fly strip and get out again on one lungful of air. There's a time for speed and efficiency; however, if you spend your whole life rushing here and there, you'll miss the little miracles of life.

Here's another look at chicken-house cleaning. You briskly walk to the chicken yard gate, slowing as the hens notice you. With the eyes of a trained detective, you look for signs of any predators that might have dug around the fences. At the same time, you observe each bird for physical problems like limps, broken beaks or any other issues. With the stealth of a spy plane you glide through the door into the coop, Yikes! A rat in the feeder! You study his sleek fur and whip-like tail. As soon as you see his beady eye, he sees you and with the squealing of his tires, if he had any, he scatters feed in all directions and disappears through an amazingly small hole in the corner. You plot his demise. The beginnings of a wasp's nest are forming above the door. Before they become a nuisance to every egg harvester, you sweep them away with a stick. When the work is finished you've sensed the state of the coop, and taken measures to improve its condition. You may have also seen the splendor of a spider web or thought about the marvel of an egg.

This second trip to the hen house may take a few extra minutes to accomplish, yet it offers a deeper experience and an opportunity to gain wisdom. You may not have the time to uncover all the mysteries of the chicken coop with each cleaning; however, if you learn to noiselessly fit into the barnyard, you'll grow in your understanding of life and be a better farmer for it.

Some men are called movers and shakers because they storm into places and get things done that nobody else can. Their skill is in using loud and forceful influences upon people and machines. Often, slower-paced folks retreat from these wild strokers and current-making kickers. The quieter ones watch from a distance and gain wisdom by seeing things movers and shakers never will.

As you learn to rest in the underwater current and have the ocean floor lay its treasures at your feet, or as you walk through a forest so quietly that its secrets open before you, you're learning to experience something greater than nature. It's a process God uses to draw you to Himself.

In an effort to restore your soul, God leads you by still waters. If you've never learned to walk by a water's edge without yelling, tearing the bark off stumps, or whacking the brush with sticks, you won't understand your Creator. There is something about being quiet that opens our way to experiencing God. The psalmist said, "Be still and know that I am God."[1]

In the oldest book of the Bible, a friend of Job gave this counsel, "Stand still and consider the wondrous works of God."[2] You won't know God's comfort, His beauty, or His salvation by running through life like your pants are on fire.

Quiet, observant hearts gain wisdom and an understanding of God that loud, hasty hearts never imagine.

Just as Ralph delights in discovering the wonders of God by silent exploration, may you experience the joy and delight God gives to those who will slow down enough to receive it.

Whoso is wise, and will observe these things,
even they shall understand the loving kindness of
the Lord.
(Psalms 107:43)

---

1. Psalm 46:10
2. Job 37:14

Questions

- Why does Ralph like to travel?

- Why did he, not his fellow divers, get to see the Christmas tree worms?

- Why does a quiet boy see more in the woods than a loud boy?

- What advice did Job's friend give him?

- What value is there in learning to be quiet and experiencing the wonders of God?

Chapter 3

A Look in the Mirror

Do we meet with unkindness from brethren?
Instead of shooting our bitter words at them,
let us judge ourselves; and endeavor, in love and
wisdom, to overcome evil with good.

—Robert Clever Chapman

"Father, would You bring people into my life that are just like me, to show me my faults?" It was a simple prayer, and I meant it. It's easier for me to see faults in others than to see them in myself. This story is one answer to that prayer.

I was working with a friend, installing the interior woodwork in new houses. One morning I arrived early, swept the room he used for a shop, and organized some of his tools. I liked him and wanted to see him get a good jump on the day. Then I cleaned my own area and began working.

He arrived after most of the men were already at their tasks. Entering the house, he met the cabinet installer. My friend told the installer that the cabinets around the fireplace didn't look right and needed to be changed. Next, he encountered the contractor

and pointed out one of her mistakes. Walking past me, he said, "I wouldn't trim a door like that."

I thought to myself, "You could at least say, 'Good morning.'"

It's wrong to seek praise, but I have to confess I wanted to hear a word of appreciation for my cleanup job. He walked into his room. I heard nothing.

I did hear God's Spirit convict me, "Forget about him. This is how *you* act when you come home from work." I didn't expect that. My co-worker was the one with the problem, not me.

The next time he walked by, he made some casual comment. Lost in thought about what God had just said to me, and still a little put out by his opening remarks, I didn't respond.

"Oh, so we are going to be moody today," he said in a sing-songy way.

I felt like picking up my tools and going home. Ten minutes ago, I had looked forward to working with him. Now, I had enough of this faultfinder. He cared more about the job than the people who worked on it. My desire to do something kind, just for him; my desire to be liked, just by him, made the whole event worse. I had looked forward to his coming, but not any more.

Within the hour we made things right and confessed our faults. He explained that he did say, "Wow," when entering the cleaned room; I just hadn't heard him. He really did care more about me than the job, though it didn't feel like it when he first showed up. We finished another day enjoying each other's company.

Driving home, I thought of the morning's events. Do I really act like that when I come home? Did I make my family wish I hadn't come, even when they had looked forward to my arrival?

In those days, my company truck doubled as the family car, depending on the time of day. I had barely arrived home when we all loaded up to go to town for groceries. My wife and daughters always liked hearing the day's news. I began telling them of my friend's arrival that morning. I had every intention of asking, "Am I like that?" Before I got the chance, my wife began laughing and interrupted, "Now you know how a wife feels!" I looked over my shoulder at my giggling daughters in the back seat.

"Am I really like that?" I asked.

My oldest daughter stopped her laughing long enough to answer, "Sometimes we meet each other on the stairs and say, 'Lie low, Daddy is in one of those moods.' We all scatter to the garden house or upstairs until later."

I mentally rehearsed one of my homecomings. Turning into the driveway, I saw a bucket on the front porch, unwatered tomatoes in the garden, and a dog's ball in the middle of the lawn. Before leaving that morning these were the only three things I had asked them to do that day. Not one was accomplished. Getting out of the truck, I asked the culprits why they failed at their assignments.

All I could think of was the bucket, the tomatoes, and the ball. I hadn't noticed the stacked wood or the weeded garden.

How did I know they had taken flowers to my ailing mother, and my favorite meal waited for me in the dining room? They looked forward to the arrival of a happy daddy. Instead they got a faultfinding man, who greeted them with questions rather than warm hugs and cheerful hellos.

I could hardly believe how blind I was to how I treated my family. They had never told me how much it hurt...or had they...and I couldn't hear it?

A finish carpenter must have an eye for mistakes. He must see things that don't line up, see things that don't close right, see things that are chipped, see things that are out of level, see things, see things, see things. His goal is to find every mistake and repair it. If he finds all the flaws and fixes them, the home owner won't see any and will be happy with his house. The finish carpenter expects to see mistakes. They're not a big deal to him. It's just part of a day's work.

When that finish carpenter comes home, it's easy to continue seeing things. At times I've viewed my home as a job site in need of fixing, rather than a nest where people love and nurture one another. From my perspective, what I say may be a casual comment—from my family's viewpoint, a devastating criticism.

God answered my prayer, and through a friend, opened my eyes to one of my blind spots. He didn't expose my problem and leave me to fix it alone. As I thought about my failure, He showed me how to get over it: *accept every task in the house and on the grounds as mine.* Mowing the lawn, cooking dinner, laundry, sweeping the porch, feeding the dogs, and everything else is my responsibility. I shouldn't expect anyone to do them but me.

When I see every task as mine, it doesn't take long for my family and me to see that I can't do it. So either it doesn't get done or somebody jumps in and helps. When somebody does what I don't have time to do, it makes me grateful. My wife becomes my helper instead of my servant. When she takes on *any* tasks around the house, she's helping me accomplish *my* work.

Someone may say this perspective is unrealistic. No one could be expected to do *every* job. But it's done so much good for our family and especially me. I wish I had seen it earlier. I rarely wash the dishes. That makes me all the more pleased with my useful daughters. I can't remember cooking a dinner. How I appreciate my wife's help! When she's doing *my* job, I can accept a meal that's half an hour "late." When would it have been on the table if I had made it? As a servant or employee, she may have fallen short. As my helper, she's done a great job of providing a faster and tastier meal than I ever could have.

I would never have learned this lesson if God had not brought my friend onto the job site as a mirror, to expose my fault. What a gift that friend has been to me.

What people in your life rub you the wrong way? Is there some critical, sloppy, tardy, or mouthy person that you face each day? Could it be that you are unaware of the same attitude or a similar trait in your own life? Next time you encounter a bothersome person, ask yourself, "What is it I don't like about them?" and then if you have the courage, ask one thing more: "God, do I act like that?"

The answer might knock you off your feet, like it did me. But the God who opens our eyes to our faults is the same God who will, with the fault, show us a way out.[1] As you follow His road of escape, you'll gain insights into all kinds of things you've never understood before.

Seeing troublesome folks as mirrors reflecting your faults is one tool that will help remove bitterness from your heart. If you can take that next step and actually thank God for sending them, you'll gain valuable wisdom, appreciation for people, and a cheerful confidence that your God is in control of this world.

> *Who can understand his errors?*
> *cleanse Thou me from secret faults.*
> (Psalm 19:12)

---

1. 1 Corinthians 10:13

Questions

- What is one reason God might bring difficult people into our lives?

- Why should you want to know your faults?

- Why are some people afraid to have their faults revealed?

- After God reveals your shortcomings, what's His next step?

- Do you have the courage to ask God to send you a mirror?

Chapter 4

Jerks

The practice of patience toward one another,
the overlooking of one another's defects, and
the bearing of one another's burdens is the most
elementary condition of all human and social
activity in the family, in the professions, and in
society.

—Lawrence G. Lovasik

For forty years I've been watching people and writing down what I've seen. Just now as I pause to look around my office shelves, I count fifty-seven journals full of experiences, biblical insights, and observances of people. As a fifteen-year-old, I began recording my findings with a simple desire to know God and His ways. My efforts have not been wasted. I'm beginning to catch on to some of the simple laws of life.

After decades of watching families, I've discovered a trait that appears in every successful home. I'm convinced that no matter how great the family, without this particular element, they will have a serious fall. The common thread running through successful families is this: There's a jerk in every one of them. Not only is there a jerk in every family, in the top notch families every member's a jerk!

The wonder of Christianity, the good news of the gospel, is that a bunch of jerks can learn to love each other. They can stick up for one another, forgive each other, and cover for the other's mistakes. A pack of jerks, under the influence of God's Spirit, lives in harmony and accomplishes many useful and good works together.

In an effort to be the perfect family, some folks won't admit that any jerks live at their address. When the curtains are closed, they argue with one another, make rude comments, and hold grudges. When the neighbors come to visit, everyone smiles and is full of fun. But, when the neighbors leave, the jerks reappear creating a ruckus.

Pride comes before a fall and keeps a family from accepting the truth that jerks live in their home. Therefore, where there are no jerks, a fall is coming.[1]

Many individuals and families have great qualities and talents. You love being around them. You can't imagine an evening of frustration with acts of selfishness displayed by the entire family—even the adults. Yet it occurs in varying degrees from house to house; it happens to all of them, at one time or another.

I haven't visited every home in the world. Nevertheless, I have read Romans 3:23 which says "All have sinned and come short of the glory of God." *Jerk* is another name for sinner. Every home is made up of a bunch of them. If you say there are no sinners at your house, you're lying or deceiving yourself.[2] On the other hand, if you honestly admit you're a jerk, you'll find God deals honestly and mercifully with you. You'll experience His forgiveness and cleansing. If you deny God's assessment that all people are jerks, you cut yourself off from His help. He doesn't like fakes and resists the proud. Therefore, a family who refuses to acknowledge their jerkery will fall.

I'm not suggesting you go out and describe all your family's failures just to prove you live with jerks. We already know that fact without you saying a word. The point is, when your

---

1. Proverbs 16:18
2. 1 John 1:8

sister acts selfishly, what did you expect? When your dad speaks sharply, why does it surprise you? There are a lot of smart sisters and many gentle dads. If you've got one of those, be glad. But what happens if your usually bright sister acts silly? Or your gentle father gets mad? Don't be surprised and, by all means, don't get upset. It only confirms that there are jerks in your home too! I imagine that you've done something silly before as well, and you've probably gotten mad at least once in your life.

In the most successful homes, every member knows that the whole bunch comes up short some time or another. If you expect everyone to be perfect, you'll be disappointed. Sure, I'd like everybody in our home to live up to a high standard, and often they do. However when they don't, I shouldn't throw up my hands in shock and look around to see if anyone outside the house saw it.

Whether you call it falling short, missing the mark, sinning, or acting like a jerk, when someone in your house wrongs you, don't take offense. Stop and consider, "What can I do for them?" In a spirit of meekness, keeping in mind that tomorrow you might be the one who needs the help, take action. Depending on the situation and your relationship to the guilty party, you might need to train, discipline, or maybe simply put an arm around their shoulder or give an encouraging word. Sometimes they might need you to step in and fix what they've broken or clean up their spill, at other times to stay in the background and pray. When you're not shocked and offended by their failures, you're free to hear God prompt you to give what they need.

Loving jerks is basic Christianity. It's God's heart. A family who loves sinners, especially those in their own home, experiences joy in the middle of problems. They know the security that comes with acceptance in the midst of failure.

As a ninth grader, I played first base on the school baseball team. I can't think of those days without laughing. Ron Fountain, our left-handed pitcher, and an outfielder named Scroggins might have had some level of respectability, but the rest of us were a cut below your average ball player.

From the beginning we knew we weren't very good, and after the first game we had to lower our opinion even further.

We regularly embarrassed our coach. Without hope of ever winning a game, we set out to have fun.

Since we knew our faults, we had to learn to help each other just to finish an inning. On a routine fly ball to Charlie in center field, the other fielders would run over in case Charlie dropped it. It was a good thing they did. I remember one time when he misjudged the ball. Instead of catching the fly in his mitt, it bounced off his forehead. Someone else picked it up and kept the runner from going to second base.

As much trouble as Charlie had catching a baseball, he could still bail out our right fielder, George Albee. During one game, I don't know where George's mind was, but his body was hunched over with his hands on his knees in the model outfielder position. *Crack.* The batter hit a high fly to right. I watched it go over my head and turned to see what George would do. He never moved a muscle. He stayed in the exact spot until the ball hit the ground about five feet from him. You should have seen him jump! It was as if someone had thrown a snake at him! Charlie was right there, though, to back him up. Even though he couldn't catch a ball in the air, he could pick one off the ground and throw it to second base, again keeping the runner on first.

We lost every game that season except one. In the final game we beat the first-place team. I don't think we had improved as ballplayers but by the end of the season, we had just learned to make up for each other's faults. It did help that Fountain pitched his best game of the year, so the rest of us didn't have as many chances to make errors.

Athletes who thought they were something special would have resented a season on our team. However, for us, we had a fun and memorable year playing baseball with guys we liked, even if we were lousy ballplayers.

The same is true with your family. If everyone expects the others to always make good plays, never make errors, and to hide it when they do, you might look like a great family on the outside—but you won't be an enjoyable team to play on.

Here's another secret for happy living. Accept that the world is full of jerks. Learn to forgive and love them with a cheerful heart, especially the ones in your own home. When they're offensive, instead of getting upset, discover what they need and provide it. If you follow this advice, you'll be doing what God is doing. And when you're doing what God is doing, you'll be happy like He is.

And don't forget, maybe tomorrow, when you're acting like a jerk, someone will use the same kindness on you that you used on them.

> *Brethren, if a man be overtaken in a fault, ye which are spiritual, restore such an one in the spirit of meekness; considering thyself, lest thou also be tempted. Bear ye one another's burdens, and so fulfill the law of Christ.*
>
> (Galatians 6:1-2)

Questions

- What have I found in every successful home?

- What happens to the families who won't admit there are jerks in their homes?

- What made our losing baseball team fun to play on?

- When you help someone who has missed the mark, what should your attitude be?

Chapter 5

Try Giving Yourself Away

*If all of us were to share our present surpluses,
we should probably find that our future needs
would be taken care of in good time.*

—David Dunn

Your Creator likes to give. It's His nature, the root of His Being. No one ever forces Him. He gives because He wants to and always gives cheerfully.

You can be sure God is a cheerful giver because He would never command us to do or be something He isn't. When you read in the Bible, "Every man according as he purposeth in his heart, so let him give; not grudgingly, or of necessity: for God loveth a cheerful giver,"[1] you can be confident that when God gives, it's always with a willing and happy heart.

One summer morning I read in Deuteronomy 26 where Moses spoke to the Israelites. He told them how to proclaim

---

1. 2 Corinthians 9:7

positively that the Lord was their God. He said when they came into the Promised Land, they should take some of the first and best fruits they found, put them in a basket, and take them to the priests. At proper times they should give them to the Levite, the stranger, the fatherless, and the widow that all might have enough food to eat. He told them to give it with their whole heart and all their soul, not grudgingly nor of necessity. Obedience to this command not only declared the Lord to be their God, it also acknowledged that He had provided all they possessed.

Through Moses, God said that if you want to acknowledge Him as God, take a portion of what He gives you and do with it what He does: give it to someone in need.

We had a bountiful garden. We also had a needy neighbor. A single mom who lived three houses down struggled to make ends meet following her recent stroke. Therefore, I decided to try what I had read in Deuteronomy.

If you want to understand the Bible, do what it says. You might gain some understanding by looking up words in a dictionary, consulting a commentary, or digging into the Greek roots. Nevertheless, there is nothing like obeying God's word to learn all kinds of things you never imagined, in ways you can never forget.

We had plenty of produce, so this wasn't any great sacrifice. The command simply meant picking a few potatoes, carrots, onions, or lettuce, putting them into a wheelbarrow, walking half a block down the sidewalk and asking, "Would you like some?"

I can't adequately describe what happened during the minutes that followed as we unloaded the food into her garage: gratefulness, joy, laughter, appreciation, uniting of hearts, tears, sharing pain, and a simple awareness of God's delight.

The wheelbarrow felt lighter as I walked back home, but not as light as my heart. I had just experienced the Living Word, and a bit of His boundless joy. It's too much for our small bodies and spirits to experience the full depths of God's happiness. Nevertheless, we can be overwhelmed with our limited portion.

I reviewed the lesson in my mind. What seemed like a musty old law was really rooted deeply in love; and love must give; and giving and happiness walk hand in hand. Therefore, what seemed like an outdated command really became a source of delight.

The *American Dictionary of the English Language* says a hobby is "a favorite object…which a person pursues with zeal or delight." For some people that might be golf, fishing, or building model airplanes. For David Dunn, the author of *Try Giving Yourself Away*, his hobby was giving. He rarely gave money. On the contrary, he focused on giving away things you couldn't buy, like smiles, confidence, or kindness. He gave away parking spaces by passing up front-row spots to take one farther away from a store entrance. He credited the cook when she provided a delicious meal. When praised, he deflected it to those responsible for helping with his achievements.

Mr. Dunn said his hobby wasn't difficult. He simply gave from the abundance found in his heart to everyday people he met. David discovered a truth about life through daily experience: giving and happiness are partners. You won't have one without the other.

My daughter has a radiant heater in her art studio. It's a disc-shaped piece of metal, with a wire coil in the center. Turn it on, the coil turns orange and sends out rays of heat. When those rays hit her skin she feels warmth. It's called radiant heat because the energy waves travel in one direction, in a ray away from the coil.

Giving and happiness are also radiant. They travel in one direction, away from themselves to needy destinations. If your happiness and giving are genuine, they are always going somewhere; you can't keep them to yourself. A giving person is happy, and a happy person automatically gives.

God's Spirit is radiant. Therefore, when a man is full of the Spirit, that Spirit must radiate out in some direction. Jesus said it this way, "He that believeth on Me, as the scripture hath said, out of his belly shall flow rivers of living water."[1]

Most people are unhappy because they attempt to get living water *into* themselves by acquiring things, instead of letting it flow out by cheerful giving. In addition, what little they do have inside, they often build a dam around in an effort to keep.

---

1. John 7:38

There's a measure of happiness in getting something you want. As Proverbs 13:12 says, "When the desire cometh it is the tree of life." Happiness is shallow, though, when it only satisfies selfish desires. The wise man sees everything that comes to him as one more gift to give away at appropriate times. If he gets a new tool, it's the chance to make something for a neighbor. If he gains a skill, it's the possibility of expanded service. When a man acquires things just for his own pleasure, he misses the greater happiness of using his possessions to benefit others.

I'm writing this chapter because I've watched many unhappy men. They've spent years trying to gain money, possessions, and fame for themselves, never realizing that happiness walks with givers, not getters. Therefore, I challenge you. Look around at your abundance. What do you have that is more than you need? Then follow John the Baptist's advice, "He that hath two coats. Let him impart to him that hath none; and he that hath meat, let him do likewise."[1] You will find happiness by giving.

I want to clarify something. After all I've said about giving and happiness, remember, happiness is not the goal. Walking with God is. If you walk with God, you'll give because He gives. You'll experience happiness because He does. Giving is just one of those practical expressions of our cheerful God. May you learn to share that part of life with Him.

As far as giving and happiness goes, don't take my word for it. Go try it; learn things you never imagined, in ways you'll never forget.

> **Then Peter said, "Silver and gold have I none; but such as I have give I thee: in the name of Jesus Christ of Nazareth rise up and walk."** (Acts 3:6)

---

1. Luke 3:11

Questions

- How do you know that God is a cheerful giver?

- What did Moses tell the people to do if they wanted to proclaim that the Lord was their God?

- What walks hand in hand with giving?

- What is a hobby?

- Do you have anything you could give away?

Chapter 6

Scaffold Wrestling

The universe has been built for us by a supremely good and orderly Creator.

—Nicolaus Copernicus

Nathan, Paul, Davey, and I stopped to enjoy our accomplishment. We had just finished installing the roof trusses on the house we were framing. It felt good to sit in the shade and drink some cold water.

The final section of vaulted trusses spanned thirty feet across the family room. They started at the top of the nine-foot exterior walls and sloped up to fifteen feet at the center. When we returned to work, Paul's job was to install two-by-four blocking between each truss at the peak to keep the trusses accurately spaced and to provide backing for the sheetrock.

We had a set of scaffolding, six feet wide and ten feet long, that barely fit under the trusses. Paul, whom we called "the Cat" because of the way he crawled around on the highest parts of the building, found every excuse he could to work on that platform high above the floor.

Vaulted trusses are sometimes called scissor trusses. If you take a pair of scissors, open them as wide as possible and then gently set the points on the floor, they look similar to a vaulted truss. You can imagine that if you have a set of scaffolding that barely fits under the trusses in the middle, it must stay right in the center, or the top corners of the scaffold will run into the bottom of one of the trusses.

This was the challenge Paul faced as he attempted to pull the scaffolding from one end of the room to the other. Keep in mind that Paul was eleven years old and weighed sixty-five pounds.

Adding to his troubles, the scaffolding had spent the last two years lying against the back side of the barn. The rusty wheels didn't roll well. One in particular required a good kick or a smack from a two by four to persuade it to align with the rest. If the scaffold moved two inches to the right of center, the top corners caught on the trusses sloping down to the right. If it moved two inches to the left, the left corners of the scaffold caught the trusses sloping down toward the left.

Paul, using every muscle in his body, began moving the scaffold. Getting off center, the front right corner caught. When he lined that up and pulled again, the back left corner, the one with the sticky wheel, went sideways and hooked on the truss above it. Back and forth he jerked and pushed. Just when he thought he had all four corners aligned to pass under the trusses, one corner would catch again.

After a few minutes of frustration, Paul began yelling and kicking as if he was in a saloon fight in an old Western town. I couldn't help but stand back and laugh. Of course, for Paul, it was no laughing matter. From his perspective that scaffold was a renegade that needed to be shot!

Though we smile at Paul's trouble, most of us have been in similar situations, though probably not with scaffolding. For us, it may have been a hose kinking under a tire as we washed the car, a cross-threaded nut, or a hard-to-reach spark plug that we couldn't seem to get a wrench on. If we don't understand what is happening, a burst of irritation is apt to steal our joy.

When God created the universe, He established natural laws that restrict all inanimate objects. An inanimate object is something that is not alive, like an extension cord or a ladder. If you pull an extension cord along behind you through a cluttered job site the plug head will usually catch on something. The laws of gravity, force, and matter, though we might not understand all of them, exert themselves upon that cord and it must obey. If the cord catches on a board nailed to the floor it will stay there unless you're stronger than the applied laws that keep it hooked. If you pull extra hard and it comes loose, the cord is not doing anything bad if it hits you in the forehead faster than you can dodge to the side. If you think to yourself, "What a no-good, lousy cord," you'd be a fool. The cord simply obeyed God's natural laws.

Let's go back to Paul's wrestling match. He would have been happy if the scaffold had quit obeying God's rules and obeyed his desire to move it through the trusses and across the room. When it continued to obey God and stay within His laws, Paul got mad.

Inside every one of us is the desire to rule as God. Some people are learning to let God be the boss in their lives, which is a restful position. Others may be able to hide their desire and only respond with slight irritation when life doesn't obey them. Some of the rest of us have experienced times when we have jerked, kicked, slammed, and thrown objects because they wouldn't do what we wanted, when we wanted it. A frustrated outburst toward any object that is simply obeying God rather than us highlights our foolishness!

Our universe is large; however, there is only enough room for one God and one set of rules. If people had the power to change the rules of the universe to fit their selfish desires, it would take only a few moments for the world to crumble into chaos.

Suppose the neighborhood bully could change nature's rules. He decides that from now on when anyone throws a cat, it will fly in a straight line like a bird, as long as nothing gets in its way. He grabs poor Tiger by the tail and after a few spins sends him flying across the park, over the river, and into the window of Roaring Rapids Pizza Parlor. Once the rest of the neighborhood boys learn about this new law, cats would be flying everywhere smashing into windows, walls, and people. Some might even make it to outer space!

Or what if a guy driving along a Portland freeway comes upon stalled traffic and makes a new law that from now on, people can drive cars right through stalled freeway traffic as if it didn't exist! Imagine the wild traffic scenes you would see then!

Suppose a man didn't want to pump water from the creek to his pasture. Instead he changed the laws of gravity so water ran uphill. By making this new law, all the rivers would overflow their banks and the ocean waves wouldn't stop at the shore. What began as a selfish wish would end in a worldwide disaster.

These are silly ideas; however, they are not any sillier than getting upset because scaffolding can't go through wood trusses or a kinked hose won't go around a tire.

If you want to be a pleasant man with a quiet heart, learn to love God's laws and submit to them. If you step on the tines of an upturned garden rake and it responds by popping you in the side of the head with its handle, instead of throwing it into a nearby blackberry patch, let it remind you that nonchangeable laws make life predictable and stable.

When the toast burns in the toaster, it is only following the law that says if you apply enough heat to bread over a long enough time, it will smoke and turn black. To wish for it to do anything else is to wish for it to disobey the order of the universe.

Proverbs 17:27 says, "...a man of understanding is of a calm spirit." The man who understands that scaffolding obeys God's ways doesn't resort to jerking, kicking, or yelling. He's free to quietly apply a lubricant to the wheels or to be patient enough to guide his equipment through tight quarters. Instead of demanding his own way, he learns to rest within the wise laws that govern the world. He knows the same law that keeps scaffolding from going through trusses keeps his Skilsaw lying on the roof instead of falling through the plywood onto the floor. His understanding earns him a reputation for having a pleasant attitude.

The next time you find yourself wanting to wrestle with some scaffolding, an engine, or maybe your computer, don't fight. Relax.

Thank God for consistent laws that make this world a predictable place to live, and learn to work within them.

Great peace have they which love thy law: and nothing shall offend them. (Psalm 119:165)

Questions

- Why did Paul attack the scaffolding?

- What would happen if everyone could make up natural laws whenever they wanted?

- If someone says you have an excellent spirit, what does that mean?

- How does understanding help a man obtain an excellent spirit?

Chapter 7

Listen, He's Speaking

The written Word is effective because, and only because, the Living Word is speaking in heaven and the Living Voice is sounding in the earth.

—A.W. Tozer, *God Tells the Man Who Cares*

This chapter contains one of the most, if not the most important lesson I could ever give to you. May God give you ears to hear.

While reading my Bible one morning I heard God speak to my heart, "Go see Lori today."

Lori lived with her parents about ninety miles away. I responded with my limited reasoning, "I can't go there. It's too far." Top speed in my 1952 Jeep was 45 mph. I didn't want to be a traffic hazard on the highway.

"Then hitchhike," He responded.

I didn't want to do that either.

His voice isn't like our voices that come and go when we open our mouths. His is just there, like a presence or gentle pressure.

I knew I had to obey. In spite of my reasoning and objections I climbed into my truck and poked my way over the Santiam Pass to Lori's.

I got there about eight, feeling a little uncomfortable at arriving so early without making prior arrangements. I knocked. Within a few moments Lori opened the door.

"How did you know to come?" she asked. "I've been crying all night and prayed that God would send someone to help me."

Last Monday while driving through Glenwood, God spoke to me, "Stop and see Chris." I responded, "If I see his truck in the parking lot, I'll pull in." I hadn't seen Chris for a year and who knows what truck he drove. I didn't see one I recognized and kept driving. Again, God's voice didn't repeat, it was just there, "Stop and see Chris."

After driving a few blocks, I turned around and went back. I had never been to Chris's business before, so I wasn't sure how to get into the building. From the parking lot I could see through a chain link fence to an open door and inside of that to a set of stairs. Timidly, I set out in that direction. Feeling like a trespasser I reached the top of the stairs. From there I saw Chris behind a desk covered with papers.

He jumped from his chair and with a warm welcome asked, "Why did you come today?"

How could I have known that his lifelong friend had been diagnosed with cancer, and at that very moment Chris needed someone to share his burden?

It is the most natural of all things for human beings to hear God's voice moment by moment. It's in His speaking and in His presence where a man finds the deepest joys, the directions for life, and the close communion that Jesus promised. Without the ability to hear God's voice, Christianity is a boring religious exercise.

For you who wonder if it's possible to actually hear God's voice, let's take a quick trip through the Bible. "In the beginning God created the heaven and the earth."[1] Why were the heavens

---

1. Genesis 1:1

and the earth created? David wrote, "The heavens *declare* the glory of God and the firmament *shows* His handiwork. Day unto day uttereth speech, night unto night showeth knowledge. There is no speech nor language where their voice is not heard."[1] Creation was a declaration by God of Himself. "For the invisible things of Him from the creation of the world are clearly seen, being understood by the things that are made, even His eternal power and Godhead; so that they are without excuse."[2]

According to the apostle John, "In the beginning was the Word and the Word was with God and the Word was God."[3]

---

1. Psalm 19:1 ff.
2. Romans 1:20
3. John 1:1

On the job site we called my friend, Paul, "the Cat," because he climbed like one. God wouldn't refer to Himself as "the Word" if He didn't speak.

Here are more examples of God's speaking to His people: (1) God talked openly with Adam and Eve. (2) To build an ark strong enough to withstand a worldwide flood, Noah had to hear specific instructions from God. (3) Abraham is the father of faith because he heard God's voice and obeyed. (4) Moses spoke face to face with God. (5) Deuteronomy is known as a book of laws. However, if you notice it's really about hearing God's voice and doing it. (6) Proverbs begs all men to hear the voice of wisdom as a guide for their affairs at home, in the business world, and in government. (7) All the prophets are examples of God's voice proclaiming His heart and will. (8) In the New Testament, Jesus, the Living Word, spoke daily in the Temple. (9) When the Holy Spirit fell upon the disciples, the first thing He did was declare the greatness of God in every man's language. (10) Throughout the record of the early church, the disciples did and said what they heard God speaking to them.[1]

God expresses Himself through nature. He has written for us a book, the Bible. He gave us a living picture of Himself through the life of Jesus. As Jesus finished that life, He said that from then on He would dwell within us by His Spirit to remind us of everything He had ever said and to show us things to come.[2] After all this, if you still need to hear His voice of instruction, the Bible says to simply ask God and He will generously give it to you.[3] What more could we need?

God's voice is not like our voice. While looking through my microscope at the fierce, amber teeth of a European ground beetle, I heard His voice. There were no words. The beauty of His design, His capacity to create textures and colors, and His attention to tiny details exalted Him in my mind far greater than words could describe. Through that beetle He told of His

---

1. For more details on the examples in this paragraph, see the following: (1) Genesis 3:8; (2) Genesis 6:13ff.; (3) Genesis 12:1; (4) Exodus 3:4; (5) Deuteronomy 4:30; 8:20; 9:23; (6) Proverbs 8:1ff.; (7) Jeremiah 1; Isaiah 6:8-9; Ezekiel 2; (8) Matthew 26:55; (9) Acts 2:4; (10) Acts 8:26,29.

2. John 16:13

3. James 1:5

goodness. He assured me of His presence. He took me out of the daily events of life and for a few minutes let me experience a small measure of His glory. He never uttered an audible word, yet, He spoke to me.

When my father-in-law told me that I needed to give more attention to writing, I knew it was God's voice speaking to me. He speaks through parents, civil authorities, bosses, and even circumstances.

Perhaps you've had a disagreement with a friend. From somewhere within you comes a prompting to go to him and humble yourself; admit your faults and overlook his. That's God's voice speaking. Often His voice is exactly opposite of what you want to do. Yet in your heart you know it's true.

Of course God speaks through the Bible. It's a treasure chest full of His perspective on life. Confidently receive it as His word to you. When you read a passage from the Bible and then specific situations come to mind where you might apply those words, usually that's God speaking to you.

Jesus said, "My sheep hear my voice."[1] He communicates throughout everyday life, in business and at home. His people hear and follow.

There are other voices. Nevertheless, the young man who diligently hides the Bible in his heart and mind will avoid strange promptings. The man who seriously desires to know God and to walk in His ways doesn't need to fear. "And when he [Jesus] putteth forth his own sheep, he goeth before them, and the sheep follow him: for they know his voice. And a stranger will they not follow, but will flee from him: for they know not the voice of strangers."[2]

I've never experienced anything greater in life than hearing and obeying God's voice. When I asked my wife to marry me she said yes. I was thrilled almost beyond measure, not because she said yes, but because it *was* God's voice all along. He had prompted and led me. He was the One who woke me in the night and told me of the future.

---

1. John 10:27
2. John 10:4-5

I'm delighted with my wife and it's not a slight to her to say that hearing God's voice and obeying Him is greater than anything I've ever experienced. It's simply placing Him in His proper place.

As the Living Word, God is always speaking. May you have the ability to hear His voice and may those words bring you the greatest possible joy this life has to offer: an awareness of His presence.

> *Behold, I stand at the door and knock: and if any man hear my voice, and open the door, I will come in to him, and sup with him, and he with me.* (Revelation 3:20)

Questions

- Why did God make the heavens and the earth?

- What are some of the ways God speaks to people?

- Why are some folks afraid to say that God speaks to people today?

- God's clearest Word has come to us through a person. Who is that person?

Chapter 8

Training Your Ears to Hear

The heights by great men gained and kept,
Were not attained by sudden flight;
But they, while their companions slept,
Were toiling upwards through the night.

—Henry Wadsworth Longfellow

POW, POW, POW; tap, tap, tap; POW, POW, POW, POW; tap, tap…tap, tap; POW, POW, POWW.

"Hey, you're out of staples! Can't you hear it?"

No I couldn't. Like any new job, there's so much to learn at once. It was my first day laying hardwood floors. I pounded on a pneumatic stapler to fasten oak boards to the sub-deck. With the help of my foot and the tap of a mallet, I'd align each board as tight as possible. Then after positioning the nail gun, I'd whack its head, which, with the help of air pressure, would sound like a small firecracker, POW. The gun shot a staple into the board, ramming it tight against the previous piece.

A good floor layer gets in a rhythm of tapping and POWING as he lays board after board across the floor. When the stapler

51

runs out of staples and the installer isn't alert, he'll think he's nailing a board when actually he's just dry-firing the gun. To an experienced layer, the sound of an empty stapler is so obvious that he can detect it even in a chaotic roomful of workers. As a beginner, I couldn't hear it at all. The instant I hit an empty shot, somebody would yell above the noise of the saw, the compressor, and the other nailers, "You're out of staples. Can't you hear it?" Eventually, I learned to hear the faint difference between a POW and a POWW, though it took longer than I would have liked.

Most professions require some ear training before a man masters his craft. When my mechanic listens to an engine, he hears all kinds of things. I hear an engine running. He hears a stuck lifter, a manifold leak, or maybe the squeak of a worn-out bearing. Within a few seconds of trying to start a car's engine, he can detect all sorts of problems just by the sound. He's learned it over time by experience.

Learning to hear God's voice is similar to learning to hear an empty stapler or an engine problem. It comes with experience, time, and paying attention.

As a young boy, the prophet Samuel heard a voice, but didn't know who it belonged to. Three times he got out of bed and went to Eli the priest, thinking he had called. Finally Eli told Samuel that it was God speaking to him. From then on, Samuel developed an ear to hear when God spoke.[1]

Hearing God's voice is not some New-Age or strange experience. It's sound wisdom and practical truth. It's basic Christianity. Jesus said He was the Good Shepherd and *His* sheep heard *His* voice.[2]

You can prepare your heart to hear and recognize the voice of God when He speaks. One of the best methods is to read your Bible. I'm not talking about three minutes a day. Read it more than any other book, more than the newspaper or your favorite magazine. Read the Old Testament stories, not as some bland historical documents but as illustrations of living principles.

---

1. 1 Samuel 3
2. John 10:3-4

Look for expressions of God's heart. Read about Jesus; learn His ways, His interests, His likes and dislikes. Gain practical insight through the letters of men who walked with Him. Saturating your mind with the Scriptures and engrafting them into your heart provides a basis for knowing the difference between God's voice and some false imitation.

When you're tempted to steal, you'll instantly recognize that it isn't God's prompting because you know what the Bible says. "Thou shalt not steal" has gone through your mind so many times that anything contrary is immediately detected and rejected. Making Scripture *yours* is one safeguard that protects you from following foolish or weird ideas.

Sarah Millard is in Mongolia. She plans to be there for at least two years learning the language. She's thrown herself into the middle of a small community she calls Yakville. I think it's a few hundred miles north of Nowhere. She eats Mongolian, sleeps Mongolian, and even washes her clothes Mongolian. All the while she's training her ears to hear the language and her mouth to repeat it. Sarah is living Mongolian and hoping for the day she can communicate the truth of Jesus with Mongolians. She would never succeed if she had stayed at home reading a Mongolian textbook, one chapter each night, before going to sleep. If it takes this much time to learn a foreign language, why should we think of giving less to understanding God's language?

Another sure way to develop your ear is to do what you already know to do. "Be ye doers of the word, and not hearers only, deceiving your own selves."[1] You'll get all mixed up if you read the Bible and then don't do it. When you do what you hear, you'll understand truth. There are no exceptions. If you refuse to obey the truth you hear, you will be deceived.

Life is one big lesson about God. Learn from everything that happens. When someone yells at you for something you didn't do, instead of getting upset ask, "What are You trying to teach me, Lord?" Take a moment, pause, listen. He might bring a verse to your mind, "If you forgive men their trespasses, your

---

1. James 1:22

heavenly Father will forgive you."[1] Maybe He'll remind you of the time you acted the same way to someone else. He might prompt you to respond kindly. Before moving on to life's next event, take time to consider, listen, and learn. He will speak to you.

God declares and shows Himself through nature. Again, take the time to ask, "What are You saying to me through this flower, bird, or ant?" Jesus said to consider how the lilies grow. One thing you will hear Him say through the lily is, "Don't worry, I will provide your clothes." Through the birds He says, "Don't worry, I will provide your food." Through the ant He

---

1. Matthew 6:14

says, "Work hard during harvest time." Everything in the universe is a preacher, a trumpet. Take the time to hear what He says through them.

The next time you consider a vacation or an afternoon of recreation, instead of running to the nearest Thrill Ville, try going to a quiet place. Observe the plants, the animals, and the sky. Ask, "What can I learn of You, Lord, from what I see, hear, and smell?" He'll speak to all who are willing to listen.

Another great way to learn to recognize God's voice is by accepting correction from whatever source it arrives. God corrects those He loves. Therefore, be confident: He will often correct you. Your parents, brothers and sisters, government authorities, laws of physics, bosses, and so on, are often God's voice returning you to His ways.

Sometimes God's voice is like a human voice. Usually it's not. His voice may sound like thunder, or be quiet and still. He might speak through the sense of His presence or a prompting, maybe like a fullness that makes you so happy you can hardly contain yourself or like an ache in your bones until you repent of your known sin. He spoke and the universe appeared. His word is the instinct of all creatures, telling the deer to give birth to fawns and robins how to build a nest.[1] Sometimes it warms the soul as it did to the two disciples on the road to Emmaus. Happy is the man who has learned to hear Him.

One chapter in this book can hardly do justice to the topic of hearing God speak. It's a lifelong adventure. Know for sure that if you can answer the telephone and within one or two words recognize the human voice of the caller, how much more should it be possible to recognize the Creator and Lover of your soul when He speaks? He promises to direct your decisions, comfort you in trials, lead you into action, and correct you when you've gone astray. How can He do that without communicating with you? It's a privilege given to every man who has ears to hear. As John says seven times in the first few chapters of Revelation, "He that hath an ear, let him hear what the Spirit saith unto the churches."[2]

---

1. Psalm 29:9
2. Revelation 2:7

May God give you the ability to hear Him and the joy that comes with an awareness of His presence, every moment of your life.

> ***Thy words were found, and I did eat them; and***
> ***thy word was unto me the joy and rejoicing of***
> ***mine heart: for I am called by thy name,***
> ***O Lord God of hosts.***
> (Jeremiah 15:16)

Questions

- How can a mechanic tell what's wrong with an engine just by listening to it?

- What does learning a foreign language and learning to hear God's voice have in common?

- How can the Bible teach you to hear God's voice?

- What does His voice sound like?

For further insights, there's a great passage in Acts 11:4-17 that describes God's voice speaking to men. Can you find an example of God speaking through a vision, a human voice, circumstances, a prompting, through reminding of something Jesus had already said, and through His Spirit taking over the mouths of men? Also notice Peter's first response to hearing God's voice and what God did about it.

Chapter 9

Why Men Don't Hear

On that two-mile walk God always talked with His servant [Rees Howells]. "I have called you friends" was no idle theory to him, but a precious and practical relationship. He always expected the Master to share these secrets with him. So as they walked that day, the Lord's word came to him again, "She will be healed and not die." "The moment I heard it," Rees said, "I had the joy of healing."

—Norman Grubb, *Rees Howells Intercessor*

Since the beginning of time God has spoken to men. All creation declares His glory. Everything He made shows His attributes. If you have the ears to hear, the heavens and the earth will tell you all about Him.[1] In addition, He has sent prophets proclaiming His heart and announcing His will. Jesus, the very image of God, also called the living Word, declared clearly the nature of the Father. When Jesus ended His days, He left His Spirit to dwell in men's hearts to remind them of everything He had said, to tell them of things to come, and to convict them of their sins.

God speaks by dreams, visions, and angels. This isn't just in stories of old. My friend Sheila recently returned from a country

---

1. Romans 1:20

where it's illegal to encourage people to believe in Christ. There God uses dreams to draw men to Himself.

The Bible records God speaking through a donkey, stars, ants, fish, birds, and even flowers in the fields. If men won't proclaim the truth, Jesus said, even the rocks will cry out. He said His voice is behind us, telling us to turn to the right or the left. His law is written in our hearts. The Bible tells us the way to live, and when we've gone astray, how to get back on the path and then guides us to stay on it in the future. And if this isn't enough, God promises that all we have to do is call upon Him and He'll tell us what we need to know.

After all this, why do so few men hear God's voice and obey Him? How can a nature lover miss the message the Creator wrote upon everything in the universe? How is it that many Bible scholars cannot hear the voice of the One who wrote the Book? Why should it be strange or difficult for a common Christian to hear and know God's voice in daily matters, especially when Jesus said, "My sheep hear my voice"?

Adam and Eve were the first people to hear God's voice. They were also the first people to reject it. Eve knew God had said not to eat the fruit. With the help of a snake, she began questioning God's word with her reasoning: the fruit was good food, pleasant to the eyes, and could make her wise. She thought it over and convinced herself to do the opposite of what she heard God say. Shortly after her disobedience, she heard the Lord's voice. In fear, she and Adam ran for cover. People today are still fearfully running and hiding from God's voice.

For a few years, I played chess on Friday nights with an elderly man down the street. Often, during our limited conversations, I'd mention something about what I had seen the Lord doing. One night he said, "I like having you come over, but from now on, leave your God at home." Mr. Nelson's heart was harder than the city street in front of his house. He had stuck his fingers in his ears and refused to hear anything God said to him. As far as I know, he remained that way until his death.

Saul set out to persecute Christians in Damascus. Jesus met him on the road, reproved him, blinded him, and told him to go on to Damascus where someone would tell him what to do next.

Then Jesus spoke to Ananias in a vision, telling him to find Saul, lay his hands on him, and heal his blindness. Ananias began reasoning and questioned the Lord's wisdom just like Eve did, "Lord, I have heard by many of this man, how much evil he hath done to thy saints at Jerusalem: And here he hath authority from the chief priests to bind all that call on thy name. But the Lord said unto him, Go thy way [in other words "do what I told you"]… And Ananias went his way, entered into the house; and [put] his hands on him…."[1] Ananias heard and faithfully obeyed God's voice. Nevertheless, he almost missed the mark as many men do. His reasoning nearly rejected God's voice. Solomon warned about this problem when he wrote, "Trust in the Lord with all thine heart; and lean not unto thine own understanding. In all thy ways acknowledge Him, and He shall direct thy paths."[2]

1. Acts 9:13-17
2. Proverbs 3:5-6

Some men hear God's voice and follow it for a while, but when the going gets tough they quit. Many grade-school or teenage boys will desire to walk in God's ways, but when they approach high school or college age the pressures of peers or of a teacher who ridicules their faith is enough to make that young man reject God's word. Then, in fear or guilt he follows Eve's example and hides from God for the rest of his life.

Worry also keeps a man from hearing and following God's voice. "I'd like you to take some of your time each morning to read the Bible and talk with Me," God prompts a young man. But the boy replies, "I'll be too tired to work if I get up early. If I can't do my job, I won't be able to buy that bike. Then in the evening, I'll be too worn out to go to Roger's house like I said I would. And I probably won't be able to stay awake in the morning anyway." We don't know what will happen in the future. Nevertheless, we often tend to imagine that what God is prompting us to do will turn out for the worse and avoid it rather than imagining how it will work for the best, and then go for it!

Here's a wiser response. "Oh, You want me to get up a half hour earlier and spend time with You, Lord? Sure, that's a great idea. I'm certain that You will keep me alert and give me the strength to do it. You'll probably give me tips on how to make the day more profitable. I imagine I'll keep out of temptations at night because I'll want to go to bed earlier. Let's start tomorrow!" The next time God speaks to that lad, you won't find him hiding in the bushes like Adam and Eve. He'll be standing confident and eagerly listening for anything his Lord might say.

Many men would rather have money coming out of their ears than God's voice going in. These men evaluate the worth of everything they hear by how much money they'll make or lose by following it. The rich young ruler couldn't follow Jesus' words because he loved his money too much.

Suppose you go to a garage sale and see your dream fishing pole standing in the corner with an eight-dollar sticker on it. What a find! As you carry your treasure to the woman collecting money at the sidewalk, you hear God prompting, "Give her the ten dollar bill in your pocket. She needs it." If you immediately respond with, "She's asking eight and I'll give her eight," your attachment to those two extra dollars just choked God's word. It prevented the Word from producing a good crop in her heart and in yours. Many folks won't hear God's voice when buying and selling because they pay more attention to the voice of money.

Ambition hinders hearing God. "I want to learn to play this instrument, go to that party, dress the best, look the coolest, have the friends…" Bent on getting what we want, when we want it, we stop His word from entering our hearts. His words seem dull when compared to our fascinating dreams.

When God speaks He plants seeds in our hearts. If we let them grow by obedience, they produce a good harvest. The boy who won't let them grow produces in his heart a crop of arguments, fights, anger, debt, drunkenness, and immorality. If you find yourself already producing a crop like that, you've gotten it by ignoring His voice.

God calls Himself the Counselor because He continually advises us concerning our motives, thoughts, words, and actions. Don't be like a stubborn mule that needs a two-by-four smacked on his head before he'll listen.

One of the greatest experiences in life is to hear God's voice. Don't let anything plug your ears.

> *For I spake not unto your fathers, nor*
> *commanded them in the day that I brought*
> *them out of the land of Egypt, concerning burnt*
> *offerings or sacrifices: But this thing commanded*
> *I them, saying, Obey my voice, and I will be your*
> *God, and ye shall be my people: and walk ye in*
> *all the ways that I have commanded you, that it*
> *may be well unto you. But they hearkened not,*
> *nor inclined their ear, but walked in the counsels*
> *and in the imagination of their evil heart, and*
> *went backward, and not forward.*
> (Jeremiah 7:22-24)

Questions

- What are some of the ways God speaks to us today?

- Why does He want to speak to us?

- What are some of the reasons men do not hear God?

- What crop is produced in the heart of men who reject God's counsel?

A true story illustrating these thoughts, is found in Jeremiah 42-44. See what Azariah, Johanan, and all the proud men did and said to the prophet. Or, if you want a New Testament parable try the Sower and the Seed found in Mark 4 or Luke 8.

Chapter 10

Look to the Root

He understood full well that the only thing that could sustain monks over the long haul was a growing relationship with God that was based on love, not fear. The regular ebb and flow of monastic life—working and praying—helped, but Bernard understood that even more important was an ongoing spiritual life in which intimacy with God was central.

—Timothy Weber, on St. Bernard of Clairvaux

There are three books I like to read: the Bible, the book of nature, and the book of life. When all three volumes clearly describe the same lesson, I know I'm beginning to understand an idea in its proper balance.

Sometimes a lesson first appears while walking in the woods. Then as I read my Bible I see it there. Maybe the next day at work some guys will act out the same message in front of me.

The lesson in this chapter began while driving to a job site. The house I'm trimming is fifty miles from home. Before leaving in the mornings, I write out a Bible verse or two in huge letters on a piece of notebook paper. Then, as I drive the freeway, with just a quick glance, I can read and meditate on those words. (I don't do this when driving in heavy traffic. On Interstate 5 at six A.M. sometimes the car in front of me is a quarter-mile or more away.)

This past week I've been considering the parable of the Sower and the Seed. "And these are they likewise which are sown on stony ground; which, when they have heard the word, immediately receive it with gladness; and have no root in themselves, and so endure but for a time: afterward, when affliction or persecution ariseth for the word's sake, immediately they are offended. And these are they which are sown among thorns; such as hear the word, and the cares of this world, and the deceitfulness of riches, and the lusts of other things entering in, choke the word, and it becometh unfruitful."[1]

While driving through Willamette Valley grass seed farms, I began thinking about roots. Where have I seen lessons about roots in nature? There was the winter when Mrs. Nelson's flowering plum tree lost a branch in a windstorm. Someone dragged it beside the garage just to get it off the sidewalk. It lay there until spring. Then on a particularly sunny day it burst into full bloom just like the rest of the tree still standing by the road! Two weeks later the blooms dried up and died. It had no root.

Each year we watch another tree topple over in a certain area of our property. These are ninety-five-year-old fir trees, some 150 feet tall. The cause is root rot. You may not detect this disease if you're just out for a walk in the woods but there's no mistake once the tree falls and its short rotten roots point toward the sky.

Our semi-dwarf cherry tree seemed to be growing nicely. Lush green leaves lined every branch. One morning we looked out the window and it appeared that George Washington had chopped it down during the night. Amazed I went out for a closer look and found it had rotted off, right at ground level.

This year we removed a few fruit trees to allow more light into the garden. Yesterday I walked out to the stumps. The plum tree had nine shoots coming from the roots. The stump remaining from the Delicious apple tree had over 125 shoots growing out of it, each twig attempting to become a tree.

---

1. Mark 4:16-19

My conclusion from nature is that poor roots cannot support healthy trees. And, as long as there is any life in a good root, it will attempt to produce a good tree.

To me, reading the book of life is when I watch people and observe the consequences of their actions. Those who attend to the roots of life do well. Those who are careless about their roots face serious problems.

In business, if you don't pay attention to the taxes you owe, if you fail to maintain your tools, keep alert to costs, and attend to customer complaints, no matter how bright the future looks, your business will show signs of sickness. Neglect these roots and your business might unexpectedly topple over some morning. Everyone will wonder, "What happened to him?" The answer will be, "He neglected the roots."

If you give all your attention to the fruit you will err. If you concentrate on the roots, fruit will appear in time. The Bible repeatedly teaches this lesson. Samuel wanted to anoint David's brother as king because of his tall, strong body. God reproved Samuel for his mistake, "Look not on his countenance or on the height of his stature; because...the Lord seeth not as man seeth; for man looketh on the outward appearance, but the Lord looketh on the heart."[1]

While driving on spring days, my wife will often say, "Look at that beautiful tree!" We'll turn our heads to see a huge ball of pink or white blossoms. Never has she said, "Look at those beautiful roots!" It takes thoughtful insight to remember that a tree's beauty springs from good roots.

Jesus taught His disciples to concentrate on the roots of their lives rather than the fruit. He said, "When thou doest alms, let not thy left hand know what thy right hand doeth: that thine alms may be in secret...when thou prayest, enter into thy closet, and when thou hast shut thy door, pray to thy Father which is in secret...[and] when you fast...anoint thine head and wash thy face; that thou appear not unto men to fast but unto thy Father which is in secret: and thy Father, which seeth in secret, shall

---

1. 1 Samuel 16:7

reward thee openly"[1] Anyone who keeps a secret root-relationship with God won't be able to hide its good effects.

Relationships are the root of every family. Families are the root of the church. Therefore when the apostle Paul wrote to Titus about establishing elders, he required that these men be married to one wife and rule well in their homes. Without home roots, churches topple over like the cherry tree in our orchard.

Nature, life, and Scripture all teach that if you want something to flourish, attend to the roots; neglect the roots, and it will likely die.

John Wesley said, "Don't look for a ministry, expect the fruit of a disciplined life." Focus on your hidden responsibilities; fruit will come.

The desire to be great, famous, and to accomplish grand things often gets in the way of true success. The pathway to a useful life is found in tending lowly roots.

"I Jesus have sent mine angel to testify unto you these things in the churches. I am the root…"[2]

If you don't grasp this lesson, your life will be a constant frustration. You'll try to do great things, see them flourish for a season, and then die. The issue is always in the root. For it is the root of the righteous that yields fruit.

I'll repeat this so you don't miss it. Jesus said, "I am the root." Proverbs tells us, "The root of the righteous yieldeth fruit."[3] If you want to be a branch that yields fruit, don't focus on the fruit. Concentrate on the secret areas of life, the places where no one sees your actions. Be diligent and faithful with the little things that only God sees. That's where you'll find the root and source of all fruit, whether in business, relationships, or the salvation of your soul.

Don't be tricked by the glamour of this world or your ambitions, regardless of how good those dreams might appear. Give attention to the roots of life and above all to the Root of your soul. Then, without struggle or frustration you'll certainly bear genuine fruit in His season.

1. Matthew 6:3-4,6,17-18
2. Revelation 22:16
3. Proverbs 12:12

*If ye walk in my statutes, and keep my
commandments, and do them: Then I will give
you rain in due season, and the land shall yield
her increase, and the trees of the field shall yield
their fruit.*

(Leviticus 26:3-4)

Questions

- Name three books that describe truth.

- Why should all three align with each other?

- Why did Mrs. Nelson's branch bloom after breaking off?
  Why did it wither?

- What does the root of the righteous do?

- Who is that Root?

Chapter 11

Picking Strawberries

*It's the sweet, simple things of life which
are the real ones after all.*

—Laura Ingalls Wilder

When I was in grade school, almost every kid in the neighborhood picked fruit to pay for their school clothes, to buy a bike, or for some distant dream, like a go-cart. I remember climbing onto an outdated school bus early in the morning with my sisters, a noisy mob of kids, and an occasional mom. The owners of huge strawberry fields in Marysville, Washington desperately needed pickers. They sent buses throughout nearby towns hoping to collect a labor force large enough to gather their fruit before it spoiled.

Though I don't recall much of what happened in the fields, I do remember a warm afternoon, pulling back the leaves and spotting the reddest, ripest, largest berry ever. I've always liked quick productive work, but at that moment everything slowed

down. Carefully pulling that beauty from the stem, my mouth began to water. Tilting back my head, I ceremoniously deposited the morsel between my teeth and gently applied pressure. The warm, sweet juice coated every part of my mouth. Can't you almost taste it?

A moment later I was back to work, picking as fast as I could and dreaming about what I'd buy with my paycheck.

My field picking days are over. Now my family has only one raised bed of strawberries. We fight deer, slugs, and the birds for every berry we get. Occasionally I'll take a bowl out to the patch and bring back a pile for breakfast or shortcake.

One day as I set out to harvest the crop, I decided to increase my productivity by pulling weeds and picking berries at the same time. Something interesting happened. As I started picking strawberries, I'd miss some of the weeds. When pulling weeds,

I'd miss strawberries. Whichever one I attended to was all my eyes could see. I could switch back and forth to some degree, but once I saw a juicy berry, that led me to another and another and…then I'd look back to see a big weed smiling at me as if to say, "You missed me, you missed me!"

As I thought about what was happening, I could hear that familiar quiet Voice in my heart saying, "The same thing happens when you look at your children. When you begin hunting for their faults, you miss their virtues. When you look at their strengths, you miss some of their flaws."

Not only was that true about my children, it applied to everyone and everything in my life. When I consider my truck, I usually think about how faithful it has been over the last 390,000 miles we've driven together. I overlook the cracked dash, wobbly steering, floppy door panel, and a long list of other things. I'm busy remembering the drives along logging roads with my family standing on the back bumper, holding onto the lumber rack like a row of firemen. I think of how it has only broken down once on the road, and that time only two miles from home. I think about the great people and the conversations we've had while driving along beautiful highways. After twenty years it's still hauling my tools to the job each day.

Lately, as I considered my troublesome carburetor, other thoughts like the oil leak, the rear brakes, and the slight bubbles under the paint at the wheel wells began to darken my perspective of the truck. I could have continued to think about a hundred other things that aren't in perfect condition. Nevertheless, it's not the time to change rigs, and therefore I choose to look on its good side.

Any dictionary will tell you that *pessimism* is the doctrine or belief that the existing world is the worst possible. A pessimist thinks that the evil in this world outweighs the good. He tends to expect the worst from every circumstance. Pessimism is the practice of looking on the dark side of things.

That same dictionary will describe *optimism* as a doctrine that believes the existing world to be the best possible. Optimists believe that good will ultimately prevail over evil. They tend to take the most hopeful view of matters, expecting the best outcome in any circumstance. Optimists practice looking on the bright side.

The apostle Paul told the Philippians not to worry when faced with troublesome situations. "Be careful [anxious] for nothing; but in everything by prayer and supplication with thanksgiving let your requests be made known unto God. And the peace of God which passeth all understanding, shall keep your hearts and minds in Christ Jesus."[1]

Most of us in America haven't experienced shipwrecks, floggings, stonings, and prison terms for doing good. Paul had, and wrote that in the middle of these adventures, he could know the peace of God because he thankfully told Him every detail of his circumstances.

He went on to challenge us to choose our thoughts carefully. "Finally, brethren, whatsoever things are true, whatsoever things are honest, whatsoever things are just, whatsoever things are pure, whatsoever things are lovely, whatsoever things are of good report; if there be any virtue, and if there be any praise, think on these things."[2]

Sadly, many of us professing Christians think and talk about the bad service we received at the restaurant, the ugly words a neighbor spoke, the false reports written in a newspaper, the weather that contradicted our plans, the man who didn't say hello when we walked by, or the society's immorality. After hours of such topics, there's no wonder we feel irritable and uptight about life.

You cannot afford to fill your mind with complaining. If you do, you'll overlook many good fruits of life. You'll be so caught up in weedy thoughts that you won't even notice when a juicy strawberry comes your way.

If you develop the bad habit of looking on the dark side of life when you're young, you won't be able to give the light and hope to friends and neighbors or wife and children when you're older. You'll see life's obstacles and miss its opportunities. When you're complaining about the gasoline prices, you won't be able to appreciate the gorgeous sunset.

---

1. Philippians 4:6-7
2. Philippians 4:8

I'm not encouraging you to become an ostrich and avoid all evil by sticking your head into the sand. The nature of life includes encountering evil. I *am* saying that you should look for the good in every situation, no matter how bleak it appears. Good is there. Look for it. If you can imagine pearls when everyone else sees only mud and oyster shells, you'll be at work gathering treasures while they worry about the incoming tides.

Just like when I was a boy, there's a great need for strawberry pickers today, men who can spot good fruit. We need men who discipline their minds to think good thoughts, who have learned to turn their cares over to God and walk in the peace that passes all understanding. These are the men who will stand tall in the days of trouble, leaders who bring hope to their families and communities.

There are times to hoe weeds out of the fields. However, I hope that you never find yourself busy attending to weeds while letting life's strawberries rot in the rows.

> *And Jesus stood still...and said, What will ye*
> *that I shall do unto you? They say unto him,*
> *Lord, that our eyes may be opened. So Jesus had*
> *compassion on them, and touched their eyes: and*
> *immediately their eyes received sight, and they*
> *followed him.*
> (Matthew 20:32-34)

Questions

- What is the difference between a pessimist and an optimist?

- Why is it hard for a pessimist to recognize good or for an optimist to see bad?

- What was one of Paul's remedies for a pessimism?

- Why is it important that fathers learn to pick strawberries instead of focusing on the weeds when dealing with their children?

- Compare a weed-picking employer to a strawberry-picking employer.

Chapter 12

Discouragement on the Willamette Pass

The fountain of content must spring up in the mind, and he who seeks happiness by changing anything but his own disposition will waste his life in fruitless efforts, and multiply the griefs which he seeks to remove. The trouble often is, we are too selfish, too unyielding in our arrangements for life's best good. Because we cannot find happiness in our own way we will not accept it in its appointed way, and so make ourselves miserable. Some excellent people are very unhappy from a kind of stubborn adherence to their settled convictions of just what they must have and what they must do to be happy. They lose sight of the fact that God rules above them, partly at least, beyond their control. They have not determined to accept life cheerfully in whatever form it may come.

—S.C. Ferguson and E.A. Allen

Do you like reading the dictionary? I do. It's not that I read it all the time; however, whenever I do it always fascinates me. When I heard that my friend Tom had been reading through the Xs, I took a look myself and used a few new words like xyster and xanthogene in my next letter to him.

Lately while looking in the Fs I came across the word *fail* which means "to desert; to disappoint; ...to neglect to give aid, supply or strength." In the following true story one father describes how he did all of the above, and God's response to him.

The date is easy to remember, July 13, 1979. My wife was ten months pregnant. There must have been some mix-up in the calculations, and now it was anybody's guess when the baby would arrive. We were tired of waiting around home for the past month, so even though our extended family campout was a hundred miles out of town, we decided to go.

My in-laws insisted I take their pickup and camper instead of our older truck and tent. We loaded up everything we could imagine and merrily drove east on Highway 58. Everything was perfect for a fun-filled vacation.

The road climbed gradually along the Willamette River. Near Salt Creek Falls it increased to a steep grade. Our engine began to sound strange. *Wahhoom, wahhoom, wahhoom.* As soon as the shoulder of the road widened enough to pull over, I stopped and turned off the engine. I didn't know what to do.

Pushing a few wires and looking for something obviously broken was the limit of my mechanical skills. Nothing helped. We waited for half an hour to let the engine cool. When we attempted to drive again, the truck lurched along and resumed its throaty growl.

This time we found a wide area to park the truck. I shut off the engine and let discouragement overcome me.

My young wife held our eighteen-month-old daughter and looked to me for hope and strength. Instead of meeting her needs, her champion caved in. Removing my shining armor, I announced, "I don't know what you're going to do, but I'm going to bed."

A camper on the back of a truck is just the thing for a sloth-ful coward. You can haul it around everywhere and simply go to sleep whenever reality becomes too hard to face. I had never had that privilege before.

Leaving my wife to care for our toddler, I crawled onto the bed over the cab. *Fail*—"to desert; to disappoint; ...to neglect to give aid, supply or strength." I had done them all.

My conscience wouldn't let me sleep. I stopped fuming about the truck and became disgusted with myself. Still, I just lay there staring at the ceiling.

I don't remember how much time passed in self-pity, when a sound sat me straight up in bed. *Wahhoom, wahhoom, wah-hoom.* A truck, running just like ours, pulled over and parked beside us. I jumped out of the camper as the driver climbed from his cab. He opened the hood of his truck, and as we stuck our noses over the radiator he said, "This happens every time I come up here. It's the air-to-fuel ratio in the carburetor."

I watched him adjust a couple of screws under the air filter. After slamming the hood and jumping back into the driver's seat, *varrooom*, his truck drove away in a cloud of dust.

I threw open the hood on my father-in-law's truck. It was exactly the same engine! An awareness of God's goodness in the face of my foolishness made me feel quite small. I humbly tightened the screws. We loaded up and our truck climbed the steep grade with ease. It ran great for the rest of the trip.

Obviously, this is NOT the way a wise man handles trials. The jerk in this story deserted, disappointed, and neglected his wife and child. He never even thought to pray for God's help. Don't you think he deserved a switching? Or at least a stern reproof?

Is that what God gave him? No. He sent a fellow traveler, who could have been an angel, to show the Failure how to repair his truck. Rather than scolding or chiding, He helped him fix the problem!

I know you want to be wise. You want to live with courage and victory, full of faith and honor. Nevertheless, there are times you will fail. At those times you need to know that even though you may have deserted God, He has not deserted you.

God is not a distant Being we must fight our way to. It's not the most talented, determined, and self-disciplined people who enjoy Him. On the contrary, the man who delights in God the most is the man who believes, in spite of his own failures, that God is, and will always be, interested in him. Certainly there are consequences for foolish actions, some of which are very serious; however, it was while we were yet sinners that Christ died for us. Therefore, while we are in the middle of failing, like the jerk beside the road, our God plans and puts into action ways to rescue us. His approach to failure is different than ours.

After bursting out with an angry word, doing something foolish, or neglecting duties, can you accept the fact that God continues to design and send good your way? If you can, you have faith in God's goodness.

I'm not talking about people who have seared their consciences, who live only for pleasure, and who think that no matter how a person lives, God will save them all in the end. I'm referring to men like the apostle Peter who wanted to die for Jesus and yet denied Him three times before the rooster crowed. Peter felt the weight of his wrong and wept bitterly. Now that he had failed, what could he do? Peter's faith caused him to repent and return at the first opportunity. He believed Jesus was still on his side, even after failure.

Jesus wasn't shocked by Peter. He knew Peter and the rest of His followers would desert Him. How did He respond to this group of failures? After His death and resurrection, Jesus met Mary at the tomb and told her to go and encourage the others. He walked along the road to Emmaus with two of them and warmed their hearts. He brought peace into a room where ten of His disciples huddled in fear. He cooked breakfast on the beach and asked them to join Him. Jesus offered comfort, encouragement, and food to the people who had recently denied even knowing Him. He is the same today; look what He did for that father along the road.

When you fail, look for Him. Surely He is on the way to meet you. Just because you've failed, just because you've "deserted, disappointed and ceased to give aid, supply or strength," don't insult God by expecting Him to act like you. Honor Him by believing that while we are yet failures, He still brings help our way.

...the goodness of the Lord leadeth thee to repentance. (Romans 2:4)

Questions

• What does *fail* mean?

• How did the jerk fail?

• What did God do when the jerk failed?

- How did Peter fail?

- How did Jesus respond to Peter's failure?

- How should we respond to people that fail us? Why?

P.S. In case you were wondering, we arrived at the campground about eleven that night, turning a two-and-a-half-hour trip into a six-hour drive due to one of my wrong turns. First thing in the morning, my wife's contractions were about five minutes apart. We did make it back to town in time for a quick delivery. On July 14, 1979, our second daughter was born to my wife and me, the jerk.

Chapter 13

The Happy 2 x 4

*The greatest need of the hour is a revived
and joyful Church...unhappy Christians are
to say the least, a poor recommendation of
the Christian Faith.*

—Martyn Lloyd-Jones

Each morning before facing the day's events, I like to read my Bible. I look for some bit of wisdom to carry with me through the predictable and surprising events that appear each day. Often, that lesson becomes a gift in my pocket, available to encourage someone I meet. My friend Bill Watkins has been a great example to me. No matter where or when I meet him, he's ready with a thought or verse to encourage me at an appropriate place in our conversation. He's able to give because he's stored up truths from his daily reading and experiences.

Life is an exciting classroom where God is my enthusiastic teacher. As I read in the morning, He usually gives me one insight or thought. Then as the day progresses He brings about circumstances to teach me how that idea relates to life. By the end of the day, if I've been alert, I've gained a little more understanding of how life works and more importantly a greater appreciation for the One who created it. You can't finish a day like that without some measure of happiness in your soul.

Frequently, a lesson carries over from one day to the next and the main idea may last a week or two as it applies to new areas, related thoughts, or verses. To help solidify the lesson, I try to write it in a journal or in a letter to a friend. If you start when you're young, and keep after it until you're old, you'll have plenty of good stories to tell about the greatness of God and His orderly and predictable universe.

Here's an example from this week. On Monday I read, "For this man [Christ Jesus] was counted worthy of more glory than Moses, inasmuch as he who hath builded the house hath more honor than the house. For every house is builded by some man; but he that built all things is God."[1]

Since I'm currently framing a house, this passage caught my attention. I took the idea to work and thought about it as we built the interior walls. That day, Davey, the eight-year-old son of the owner and a member of my framing crew, wanted to be the boss instead of the happy worker. He would have never *said* that he wanted to be the boss; however, by his actions he showed he wasn't going to be happy unless things went his way. Each job I assigned him produced much whining and little action.

While watching Davey, it dawned on me: this was a living picture of the verses I had read earlier that morning. I kept a lookout for the complete lesson.

We use studs to build walls. Studs are two-by-four or two-by-six pieces of wood all cut the exact length to reach from the floor plate to the ceiling plate. We nail them vertically every sixteen inches along the wall except at doors or windows. Plywood attaches to the outside and sheetrock to the inside.

God is building a house and using us for studs. He chooses to nail us into whatever wall He wants. It's a privilege to be the slightest part of that house, but sadly many of us whine and complain just like Davey, because we are not placed where *we* want to be.

---

1. Hebrews 3:3-4

Most of us want an important place, like near the front door so others can see our greatness. The mother of James and John wanted her sons in that position when she asked Jesus, "Grant that these my two sons may sit, the one on thy right hand, and the other on thy left, in thy kingdom." Jesus replied, "...to sit on my right hand, and on my left, is not mine to give, but it shall be given to them for whom it is prepared of my Father."[1]

God has a spot prepared in this life and in the life to come for each of us. He will nail us in the best possible place for His glory. We might as well get used to it—you and I are not the center of the universe. Life doesn't revolve around us. Instead of trying to be someone spectacular for God, we would be better off, and surely more content, by simply enjoying where He places us. Have you ever heard that song, "Brighten the corner where you are"?

Imagine walking into a huge house framed with two million studs. Suppose each stud had the ability to speak and with the exception of two or three all complained about their positions continually. "I don't like it here! I want to be by the window! I want to be next to him! Don't put me here! It's not fair; the cedar board is above the fireplace." What an obnoxious racket that would be! If you were the builder it might be enough to make you tear the house down and start over.

That's how God felt when He led the house of Israel from Egypt to the Promised Land. Almost every one of those two million Israelites complained and griped about whatever God did or wherever He led them.

What did God do? He opened the ground and a few thousand disappeared into it. He sent snakes to bite them and gave Miriam leprosy. He let them wander around until all the complainers died. The few that didn't complain He saved for a future house where there would be no complaining.

God's people have continued to complain since the days of Moses. Here's a quote by William Law, written in 1730, as he considered the Christian community of his day, "Need a man do more to make his soul unfit for the mercy of God than by being

---

1. Matthew 20:21,23

greedy and ambitious of honor? Yet how can a man renounce this temper without renouncing the spirit and temper of the [Christian] world in which you now live."[1]

Those who want glory and honor must steal it from God. Remember, it's the Builder who deserves the honor, not the house itself. It would be foolish for a two-by-four to cry out, "Honor me! Honor me! I'm more important than the Builder!" It's just as foolish for us to desire honor in God's house.

---

1. William Law, *Wholly for God,* edited by Andrew Murray (Minneapolis: Bethany House Publishers, 1976).

Imagine what it would be like to walk into a house framed with millions of studs and find every one of them content in their assigned place. If they could talk, you might hear something like this, "Oh thank You Lord for nailing me here! You're the greatest Builder! Thanks for letting me be a part of Your project!" Wouldn't you like living in a house like that? That's the way to honor a good Builder.

After we had a few conversations, Davey caught the message found in Hebrews 3, which was: Be a happy stud in God's house no matter where you're nailed. He began walking through each room with his carpenter pencil, drawing happy faces on every stud, rafter, and joist he could reach. He obeyed me and the whole crew was happy for that!

Life offers joy to the man who rests contentedly where God has nailed him. He has picked your time in history, the country of your birth, your parents, your brothers and sisters, your gender and even the day of your death. If you complain and refuse to thank God for these nonnegotiable parts of life, you're like a whining two-by-four who thinks you're wiser than your Builder. It's not only complete foolishness. It's rebellion.

God is building a happy house where there will be no whiners. Your particular place is where you are today. If you can't be happy there, you won't be happy should your location change. True happiness comes from within, not from your situation. Accept your place, quit complaining, and rejoice to the end for the spot you already have in His house.

There you have today's lesson. I wonder what tomorrow's verse will be and what experiences God will use to make it come alive.

But Christ as a son over his own house; whose house are we, if we hold fast the confidence and the rejoicing of the hope firm unto the end.
(Hebrews 3:6)

Questions

- What's one thing I like about Bill Watkins?

- What was Davey's problem?

- What did he do that showed he got over it?

- Name a few unchangeable parts of your life.

- If you try to get honor for yourself, who do you have to steal it from to get it? Why?

Chapter 14

Squirreling

Do you admire Aquila and Priscilla, Paul's "helpers in Christ Jesus,"
and who were so skilful in the Scriptures, that they were able to
teach a young minister the way of God more perfectly? You will find
that one reason for their familiarity with the Scriptures was, that
they had a "church in their house." It was doubtless recognized
in regard to spiritual as well as in regard to temporal things, that
"if any provide not for his own, and especially for those of his own
household, he hath denied the faith, and is worse than an infidel."

—J.W. Alexander, *Thoughts on Family Worship*

Have you experienced feeling like a squirrel? That's the term we use around our home to describe the joy that comes when the fruits of a harvest are safely put on the canning shelves, packed in the freezer, or stacked in the woodshed. When a man has taken advantage of the season and gathered some product that will make life easier during another time of the year, he experiences the "happy squirrel" sensation.

The feeling comes when the last chicken has been butchered, cleaned, placed in a bag, and the lid of the freezer shut with a thump. Your body's tired. You're glad it's over. There's a sense of victory and of a challenge overcome. What's more, there's the picture in your mind of baked chicken on a rainy November night.

I get that squirrel feeling after picking the orchard, when the onions are braided and hung to dry, or on the way home from the canned-food case sale. Of course, an all-day drive to Klamath Falls to pick up a year's worth of potatoes with my friend Will ranks nearly tops on the squirreling chart.

Squirreling isn't easy. Fingers numb from handling frozen fish and the overpowering smell from a pressure cooker are simply part of the tuna-canning process. Picking blackberries is usually hot and prickly work. Gathering cucumbers for pickles and tomatoes for sauce often brings on a sore back. Nevertheless, it's all worth it when the day's done. When you stop to look at your store, it's the squirrel feeling that makes you smile.

Most folks don't get the privilege of feeling like the squirrel who laid up enough nuts to last the winter. Many work to get enough money to buy what they need for a day or a week at a time. They miss the sense of seasonally gathering provisions. Canning is left to the cannery and purchased from a store. Fishing is left to a commercial company and bought over the counter. Life's experiences are often limited to eight-to-five jobs, getting a paycheck, and paying someone else to squirrel for them.

When all you get at the end of the day is money to pay for something bought with a credit card last year, the joy of work diminishes. There's a big difference in working to pay off a loan from the past and working to save for something in the future. In the first case you're a slave, working because you have to. In the second, you're a free man choosing to work, preparing for something to come.

Even so, with the right perspective, working a daily job can be a squirrel experience by gathering up funds for the future. Hard work and economy allow a man to collect a measure of resources to meet unforeseen needs.

Larry works a regular job, yet he still makes time for great squirreling adventures. For his vacation, Larry traveled to the Oregon coast. There, he camped and fished with extended family members. After hauling in their catch, they set up the pressure cookers and propane burners to can those fish right there in the campground. Not only did they benefit from a scenic vacation, they returned with a year's supply of seafood.

When our neighbor Mrs. Nelson was a girl, their family climbed into a wagon each fall and drove their horses up the McKenzie River valley. Camping for a week beside the river, they picked blackberries and made jams, jellies and pie fillings over the open fire.

There's a place for water skiing and dune-buggy-riding vacations. However, if you're looking for ways to enjoy life, consider squirrel outings. Then, when the weekend is over, you've not only had a great time in a beautiful setting with the folks you love, you also return with useful resources for the winter ahead.

The goal of squirreling isn't to obtain a hoard of supplies. The goal is to lay up, ahead of time, the resources for approaching needs and even a little extra to give away. Paul's advice to the new Christians in Ephesus was "Let him that stole steal no more:

but rather let him labor, working with his hands the thing which is good, that he may have to give to him that needeth."[1]

When our girls were young, we found an abandoned Italian plum orchard. After obtaining permission, we gathered over fifty gallons of plums. We had enough to can, dry, eat fresh, and give away. Months later, we still had bags of dried plums to take on outings and share with friends. Those family trips to gather plums and the squirrel feeling we shared are great memories.

As a young man, you might not have a lot of money to help around the home and maybe you're a little bored during the summer. That's the perfect time to look for opportunities. Is there an apple tree that nobody wants to pick? Are berries growing along the roadside? Maybe somebody's vegetable garden overproduced and the owners have green beans coming out their ears. These are God's gifts to you, just as nuts are His gifts to diligent squirrels. It's an opportunity to gather and store what you've harvested. Canning, freezing, drying, and tending a smoker are all fascinating skills that many men have never acquired.

Do you know how to harvest, cook, or preserve food? I'm not talking about buying it at the supermarket and popping it into a microwave oven. Many of life's greatest memories are tied to harvesting, preparing, and eating food with family and friends. The man skilled in these areas is a great asset to any group. His efforts bring joy to many people and put happiness in his own heart.

God designed men to sense pleasure when they work at the basic responsibilities of life, like providing food for a household. Accepted as a privilege rather than a burden, every diligent man has the opportunity to experience that "happy squirrel" feeling as he gathers God's gifts for his family, and as a resource to give away.

Who then is that faithful and wise steward,
whom his lord shall make ruler over his household,
to give them their portion of meat in due season?

---

1. Ephesians 4:28

Blessed is that servant, whom his lord when he cometh shall find so doing. Of a truth I say unto you, that he will make him ruler over all that he hath.

(Luke 12:42-44)

Questions

- Why do squirrels gather and store nuts?

- What kinds of things do people gather and store?

- Should people only gather just enough resources for themselves?

- Why does a man feel happy when he has finished filling the woodshed with wood?

P.S. I've got a date with my wife this evening: Blackberry picking at the Waterville Reservoir!

Chapter 15

Tests

Taking the SAT is like going to the doctor. It scares the willies out of you, but once you get there it's really not that bad, and in the end it's all for the best.

Today, after a year of studying, my daughter faces the national paralegal examination. "Are you nervous?" I asked.

"I'm not nervous," she replied. "I'm excited."

"Do you like taking tests?"

She smiled and nodded her head.

From the age of seven until they were teenagers, our children took annual academic achievement tests. Before every examination I gave them a pep talk. "I don't care if you flunk the test. It doesn't matter to me if you miss every problem. The important thing is that you have a good time. Go and enjoy it."

Accurate tests reveal truth. I wasn't afraid of what the scholastic tests revealed about my children. I didn't want them to fear either. A poor score simply meant they either needed more study on a certain subject or a lesson on how to take a test. The results weren't important; enjoying the examination was. Life brings one test after another; if you don't like tests, you won't enjoy life.

It's time for a surprise arithmetic quiz. Do the following math problems in your mind: Multiply 40 times 25...divide 36 by 4...add 3/16 to 7/8... Does the very word *quiz* make you nervous? Are you embarrassed by your math skills? Or, do you know the answers as soon as you hear the questions? By taking this quiz you discover, if you didn't know already, something about your arithmetic abilities and your attitude about examinations. The test reveals truth about you.

Christians claim to love truth. It's easy to love the truth about your math skills when you can accurately solve those problems in the blink of an eye. But, what if you can't? How do you feel then? How can you love truth and like tests when they reveal your ignorance or your faults?

By learning the answer to this question and applying it to future tests, you'll avoid hours of worry, gain remarkable wisdom, and develop the skill to cheerfully face any trial or test that crowds into your life.

How can you like tests that reveal your shortcomings? The answer is simple. Learn to love truth. Love it no matter how it makes you look. Love it regardless of where it may lead you. You'll find freedom as you learn to love truth.

A friend of mine owns a sailboat. Years ago he feared flipping his boat and wondered if he could right it again if he did. One blustery day tested his skill. The wind dumped him into the lake fifteen times! Through those humbling experiences he now knows the truth: it's not that hard to right his sailboat. He's not afraid anymore. The test revealed the truth and knowing the truth freed him from fear.

Danny takes his driving test tomorrow. If he doesn't pass, he can't drive. If he can't drive, he can't get that job he wants. Imagining the future should he fail makes him nervous and afraid. When we care more about our plans and circumstances than we do about truth, it's easy to become fearful and stressed. If Danny loved truth he'd look forward to tomorrow's driving test. Then he'll know whether he needs more practice or if it's time to drive the roads alone. A truth-lover welcomes tests and accepts results.

Pride avoids both tests and truth. Pride would rather lie to look special than face the reality of being average or uneducated. When loving truth sets you free, you welcome the tests even when they expose your lack of knowledge. Open ignorance is better than the concealed ignorance because open ignorance is easily overcome, while hidden ignorance remains.

Let me explain. On a job last week one worker arrived and said, "I've never done this before." Immediately, I set out to teach him everything I knew about the task. Another worker arrived saying he could do it all. With a sense that he really couldn't, I backed away from him in my heart, kept my advice to myself, and waited for the tests of work to expose the truth. Throughout the day those tests revealed that though he did have some knowledge, he lacked more than he realized. After noon, he began admitting what he didn't know and asked for help. Immediately, I set out to teach him.

Don't be afraid of life's tests revealing your ignorance. The sooner you realize and accept the truth, the sooner you'll gain knowledge and wisdom.

Though tests prove all kinds of truth, the two most important truths daily tests reveal are: first, you need God, and second, God is willing to meet your need.

Every trial, test, and trouble you face is a friend declaring truth about yourself and God, about your need and His ability to meet that need.

I'm not afraid of thieves stealing my things because I've had all my carpentry tools stolen. I saw God turn what looked like a bad event into two of the happiest months of my life. I took a logging job until I could afford to buy tools again.

While on vacation we watched God amazingly recover our car after thieves stole it from the motel parking lot. The police said we'd never see it again, yet we had it back before we needed it.

I'm not worried about running out of food. I've stood in my kitchen without even one crumb to eat. With miraculous timing, God bountifully met my need. The test revealed that I need food and God provides it.

If you knew that having your tools stolen, your car stolen, and running out of food would increase your faith in God and provide a thrilling and unforgettable experience with Him, wouldn't you want it? Today, you might honestly answer, "No I wouldn't want it." Nevertheless, I hope the day comes when your confidence in God and your deep desire to experience Him will allow you to rejoice at the beginning and in the middle of trials and tests.

That's why when James, the brother of Jesus, wanted to give practical instruction to early Christians, his first piece of advice was, "My brethren, count it all joy when you fall into divers [various] temptations."[1] He didn't say fight your way through it and after you see the super outcome rejoice. His advice was, "Count it joy while you are in it." Before you see the good.

Until you develop eyes to see trials as the pathway to knowing and trusting God, your life will be one irritation after another. You'll be caught complaining about the tests instead of rejoicing in the opportunities to learn what's true. Whining about tests confirms you're more focused on you, rather than on the truth.

Suppose you're standing in the kitchen looking at an open container of chocolate-covered almonds. You would like to eat one; however, your mom said, "Don't eat any until after dinner." There's a tension in your mind—you want to eat one, but you shouldn't. This is a test. The following moments will reveal facts about you. Are you an obedient boy who has, by God's grace, control over his desires? Or, are you a slave to various lusts and pleasant feelings? The issue isn't whether you eat the chocolate and almonds; they're just the test. The real issue is what kind of heart do you have?

Chocolate almonds may be a challenge to some people, but they are trite compared to what many folks face each day. The list is endless: angry neighbors, serious injuries, an offer to smoke,

---

1. James 1:2

death of a friend, a temptation to steal, or challenging sisters. These are the diverse temptations that James says to acccpt joyfully. The particular test isn't important. What the test reveals about you and about God is.

While God proves us, He likes us to test Him. "Bring ye all the tithes into the storehouse, that there may be meat in mine house, and prove me now herewith, saith the Lord of hosts, if I will not open you the windows of heaven, and pour you out a blessing, that there shall not be room enough to receive it."[1] God challenged Israel to test Him that the truth might be known.

King David gave this dare: "O taste and see that the Lord is good."[2] He didn't want you to take his word for it. Test God yourself. He's not afraid of truth.

Every time you read something in the Bible and determine to live it, you're testing God. For example, in Proverbs we read, "Seest thou a man diligent in his business? he shall stand before kings; he shall not stand before mean [insignifcant] men."[3] If you purpose to diligently apply yourself to whatever business you enter and observe what happens, you'll be a living test, proving the truth of that verse. Don't rely on other people when it comes to knowing God. Get your own first-hand experiences. Test His word by living it.

You can't love God without knowing Him. You can't know Him without experiencing Him. You can't experience Him without experiments. Therefore, when all kinds of tests and trials push their way into your life, don't treat them as enemies, greet them as friends.

Whatever tests you face today, whether in law, math, or in the adventures of life, for the love of truth, enjoy them.

But we glory in tribulations also:
knowing that tribulation worketh patience; and
patience, experience; and experience, hope: and
hope maketh not ashamed; because the love of

1. Malachi 3:10
2. Psalm 34:8
3. Proverbs 22:29

God is shed abroad in our hearts by the Holy Ghost which is given unto us.
(Romans 5:3-5)

Questions

- What do good tests reveal?

- Why do many people not like tests?

- Why does God like trials and tests?

- Why does our pride avoid tests?

- What should our attitude be when trials come our way? Why?

For further study, get a concordance and look at all the times Ezekiel writes, "Ye shall know that I am the Lord." Discover what things bring the knowledge of God.

Chapter 16

Judgments

Judge not the Lord by feeble sense,
But trust Him for His grace;
Behind a frowning providence
He hides a smiling face.

—William Cowper

If you want to live in joy and rest, you must believe that God controls the judgments men place upon you. Whether they praise or curse, accept the verdict as God's best. It's not that God simply allows people to curse or praise you; He often prompts them. Can you believe God purposely brings angry, mean, and hard-hearted people into your life, and at times, places them in positions of authority over you? If so, you've learned one secret to a happy life.

The man who won't believe God controls the judgments he receives often lives under a dark and heavy cloud. His mind fills with irritating thoughts toward those who, from his perspective, treat him unjustly. If someone misunderstands or speaks ill of him, he views them as a problem or an enemy rather than God's servant and messenger. While concentrating on what seems bad, he misses what is good. When he should be rejoicing and resting in the best, he's grumbling against it.

My daughter entered a painting in the local mayor's art show. As she left home for the awards presentation, I reminded her of the words in Proverbs, " 'Many seek the ruler's favor, but every man's judgment is from the Lord.'[1] Accept what the judges say as God's verdict for you." She smiled and said she would.

It's hard to anticipate the decisions of an art judge. A poorly painted portrait of a long-necked, ludicrous lady won first prize in her division. Second and third places seemed questionable also. The honorable mention went to a talented artist. The judges, looking for modern and not traditional art, didn't recognize my daughter's work at all. A judge has the right to pick what he or she deems best. With her heart accepting the results as from God, she thanked Him.

A Wisconsin art supply company judged the picture differently. They gave her a large ribbon and a gift certificate for $150 worth of art supplies. A woman from the hosting art guild gave her a member's award of $25. She received ten other cash awards from gallery visitors. My daughter returned home with the happy assurance that all her judgments came from God, the failure to place as well as the gifts.

As my Little League baseball coach, Dad taught me to play first base. I enjoyed playing, especially since he had given me the skills to play well. When I turned out for the high school team the coach told me, "We don't play right-handed first baseman. We use only lefties." I didn't see the value at the time. Nevertheless, the coach's judgment took me out of high school sports and turned my interests into more useful avenues.

The Bible is full of examples attempting to teach us the principle that God controls the judgments we receive. Those in authority over us may make a mistake, respond in anger, or do something obviously foolish, yet God uses it for our best.

As King David left Jerusalem, fleeing from his rebellious son, a man named Shimei walked parallel to him. From a distance

---

1. Proverbs 29:26

he threw rocks and cursed. David's men requested permission to remove Shimei's head. David reproved those servants with these words, "Let him curse, because the Lord hath said unto him, Curse David…let him alone, and let him curse; for the Lord hath bidden him. It may be that the Lord will look on mine affliction, and that the Lord will requite me good for his cursing this day."[1]

No one would have blamed David for killing that cursing Shimei. Nevertheless, David trusted his God. Either he had the curse coming or God would use it for some future good.

Pharaoh was a wicked ruler. He placed nearly impossible workloads upon the Israelites, changed his mind regularly, and failed to keep his promises. When he did let the people go, God led them by Moses to the Red Sea shores where they could be easily trapped. Then the Lord hardened Pharaoh's heart, who chased after them.[2] In the end, God saved Israel by opening the sea whereby Israel escaped, the Egyptians perished, and everyone knew the Lord was God.

Throughout the Old Testament, God changed the minds of authorities to lead and teach His people. Sometimes He would reprove foreign kings and not let them harm Israel. At other times, He prompted those same kings to hate His people and deal subtly with them. When Israel rebelled, He gave them into the hand of the heathen. When they confessed their errors, He made their captors pity them.

God controls authorities today just as He did in the Old Testament days; He's the God of current events! The president's heart is in the hand of the Lord and He changes it whenever He wants. God rules over North Korea, Iraq, and the United States. He hardens hearts; He prompts with mercy; He controls world affairs for one purpose: That all people may know that He is the Lord.

When the devil entered Judas and prompted him to betray Jesus, God didn't wring His hands saying, "O, what should I do, what should I do?" God is no weakling. Selfish and wicked wills

---

1. 2 Samuel 16:11-12
2. Exodus 14

cannot damage His plans. When Jewish leaders and Pilate condemned Him to die, Jesus received the judgment as from His Father, not as the whims of evil men. If the devil and his princes had known what was happening, they would have never crucified the Lord of Glory.[1] They attempted evil, but God used it to accomplish the greatest act of love ever performed on earth. In addition, He used angry, hateful, and even demonic leaders to accomplish the task.

If God is going to use wicked men to complete the most wonderful event ever, can't you trust Him to work on your behalf through the judgments you receive, even when they come from foolish or mean authorities?

When an angry boss gives you a hard assignment, accept it as God's best. Dive into it with your whole heart. When an overworked policeman gives you a driving ticket and he's not as polite as you think he should be, don't complain about his shortcomings. Receive the reproof as from God's hand. Show up in court. Accept the judge's decision. Pay what he requires.

A certain woman recently received a ticket after speeding in a school zone. She went to court. The judge upheld the ticket and assigned a fine. The next woman before the judge committed the same crime. He let her go free. Both cases looked identical. As the first woman paid her fine, she retained her joy with the assurance it was her God Who gave the judgment, not simply a person behind the bench.

Our judgments don't come out of nowhere by the random wills of men. Our promotion doesn't arrive from the east or the west or even from the south. God is judge. He puts down one and sets up another.[2]

If you accept all the judgments you receive as God's best, you're free to be happy and content. Thankfulness and praise will wash the griping and complaining out of your mind. It's one of those secrets few men learn to enjoy.

May you be one of those few who live in rest and happiness simply because you believe that your God controls all judgments.

---

1. 1 Corinthians 2:8
2. Psalm 76:6-7

*Many seek the rulers' favor but every man's
judgment is from the Lord.*
(Proverbs 29:26)

Questions

- Does God ever harden the hearts of men so that they do what appears to be mean things?

- Why would He do such a thing?

- Do you believe that God controls the decisions of current world leaders?

- When a man receives a promotion, who gives it to him?

- When a man receives a demotion, who is behind it?

- What is one reason why few men live happy and restful lives?

Chapter 17

A Time to Give

Those who bring sunshine into the lives of others cannot keep it from themselves.

—James M. Barrie

If you're ever in Springfield, Oregon and you want to experience a man's store, head for Roberts Supply. It's next to the railroad tracks near the corner of 28th and Main. They've got everything for the man who works outdoors: rugged clothes, boots, rain gear, safety equipment, axes, tree climbing spurs and all kinds of logging supplies. Even if you're not planning on buying anything, it's a great place to browse around.

Sometimes, during the hot days of summer, they've been known to fill a washtub full of ice and cans of soda or lemonade. You could have one for free. It was right generous of 'em.

Giving out a cold drink is a small thing. Nevertheless, I can still remember a particularly hot afternoon, after ten hours of chasing behind a bulldozer, walking into Roberts and seeing those cold drinks, packed in ice, just waiting for me. For probably less than fifty cents a can, they gave me a memory that will last a lifetime.

Generous folks don't have to give much to impact somebody's life, just a little more than what's required.

Generosity is a pleasing and remarkable quality because it's the nature of God. Deep within each of us is a longing for His attributes. If we haven't completely rejected Him and for some foolish reason hate His guts, we'll experience pleasure whenever we see a generous act, because it's an expression of the One for whom our heart longs.

God has all He needs. He enjoys freely giving to people more than they need. He's never stingy. So when it comes to time, you can be sure that He has given you all the time you need to accomplish all He requires, and then a little extra. Many folks complain they don't have enough time, never realizing that since it's God who gives time, He's the One they're griping about. It's like when folks complain about the weather—since God determines it, every complaint is aimed at Him. The truth is: He's given us more than enough time to finish what we need to do in our lives.

Since God is generous with time, and since we are created in His image, we are free to be generous with the time He has given us. That doesn't mean that we can give away all we have. If Roberts Supply, in addition to offering pop, began giving away everything in their store, before long they wouldn't have anything left to sell! They've chosen to give away a realistic portion of their abundance to brighten the lives of customers like me.

Likewise, you have a small abundance of time to invest. Your investments will make life more enjoyable for you and for those God brings into the store of your life. Unlike money and talents, every person gets the same amount of time each day. The Prime Minister of New Zealand gets twenty-four hours, just like the grade-school boy in Malaysia. All of us have a little more than we need and therefore all have the privilege of investing it in our world. It's possible to take our little extra and transform barren patches of life into beautiful and productive gardens.

Here's how you do it. If you're required to work on a math assignment for twenty minutes a day, experiment with generosity and give twenty-two minutes. See how much you can accomplish in those additional two minutes. Don't do it because you have to, but because you've chosen to invest a gift of time into learning math.

If you're asked to clean the kitchen for five minutes, faithfully fulfill the requirement; then give sixty more seconds to the job. You normally won't have three more hours to give to cleaning the kitchen, but you usually can find one more minute to invest, and that one minute is enough to change your whole attitude and to make your mom's day.

If you're old enough to drive and it takes fifteen minutes to travel to an appointment, work, or a meeting, try giving twenty. With five extra minutes to give, you're free to let your neighbor have one minute by a momentary stop at the mailbox to say hello. On another occasion you may give three minutes to a stalled motorist by helping him push his car out of the intersection. You normally won't have the time to rebuild his engine by the roadside because of your prior commitments, but those few minutes of kindness, given to help him to safety, meet his immediate need.

In the event that you drove straight to the appointment without any chances for generosity, arriving early offers all kinds of opportunities. Maybe you could help set up, or have time to greet someone with more than a quick hello before getting down to business.

Men who invest minutes here and there into everyday events meet new people, cheer up lives, remove obstacles, and turn routine jobs into memorable experiences. It's those extra minutes that give you something to talk about. They transform you from a beggar, who is always late and wasting other people's time, into a wealthy man with useful moments to spare.

When we sit as a family at the evening meal and recount the noteworthy events of the day, the highlights are almost always the extra moments we've invested in the lives of people or the minutes others have invested in us. I'm confident that if you consider it, you'll find the same true for you.

For many people, life is becoming faster every day. Evenings fill with one activity after another. Eight-hour jobs spread into overtime. Weekend responsibilities increase until the signboard of their souls lights up like the red sign at an overbooked motel, SORRY, NO VACANCY.

When God gave us the hours for each day, He never intended us to use it all on necessities or selfish pleasures. He provided and still offers an abundant life. It's a life with enough time for our assignments and some to give away.

Therefore, if you want to live a full and bountiful life, when possible, arrange your events so that you may give the time required for each, and then just a little more.

Your actions will create memories for yourselves and others to last for decades. That's what Roberts Supply did for me with a cold fifty-cent can of pop on a hot day.

Listen to what Solomon had to say about time. "To every thing there is a season, and a time to every purpose under the heaven: A time to be born, and a time to die; a time to plant, and a time to pluck up that which is planted; a time to kill, and a time to heal; a time to break down, and a time to build up; a time to weep; and a time to laugh; a time to mourn, and a time to dance; a time to cast away stones, and a time to gather stones together; a time to embrace, and a time to refrain from embracing; a time to get, and a time to lose; a time to keep, and a time to cast away; a time to rend and a time to sew; a time to keep silence, and a time to speak; a time to love, and a time to hate; a time of war, and a time of peace."[1] Doesn't it sound like God has allotted enough time to do all that a man must accomplish in his life?

May you be that wise and wealthy man who manages his time that he might give generously to each required event and a little extra for the life in between. It's the nature of God and the longing of your soul.

> *But this I say, He which soweth sparingly*
> *shall reap also sparingly; and he which soweth*
> *bountifully shall reap also bountifully. Every man*

---

1. Ecclesiastes 3:1-8

according as he purposeth in his heart, so let him give; not grudgingly, or of necessity: for God loveth a cheerful giver. (2 Corinthians 9:6-7)

Questions

- What did Roberts Supply give away?

- Why did such a little gift make a lasting memory?

- Why do little moments of time often create the highlights of the day?

- If God has given us all the time we need, and if we always feel like we don't have enough time, what's wrong? How can we change it?

Chapter 18

Bringing Home the Light

Any and every duty is undertaken cheerfully and willingly and no complaint or whining is ever heard no matter what hardships or inconvenience may be encountered. The principal credit of this is due to the tact and leadership of the head of the expedition and the cheery happiness and bonhomie [good nature] of Wild. They both command respect, confidence and affection.

—Frank Worsley, Captain of the *Endurance*

Have you ever entered a dark garage or hiked alone through a forest at midnight? These might be familiar areas in the daytime, places where you've experienced many happy times. Nevertheless, turn off the fluorescent lights or have the sun go down and the whole atmosphere changes.

What was that noise? I thought I heard a growl. Without being able to see the source of sounds, our minds sometimes imagine the worst. Our eyes resemble baseballs for size and the hair on our necks makes us look like a porcupine. At times we might even feel the end is near!

With a flick of a switch, the garage lights reveal a cat rubbing his side on the shovel in the corner. "Oh, it's just you, Morris," you say with a chuckle of relief.

With the rising sun, the scary wilderness shapes and sounds become inspirations. "Lord, what a beautiful forest You've made."

What turned a fearful sound into laughter at a cat and a nervous night hike into a relaxed walk of praise? Simple light. Light brings understanding and the man of understanding is of an excellent spirit.[1] His fears disappear and he's free to cheerfully go about his business.

For many people, the world is a dark place. It's full of uncertainties and questions: Why are there wars? Is someone going to steal my things? Will I have enough money for food? Will there be a job for me when I get older? What about the wickedness the news talks about? Why is my sister sick? What's the meaning of life anyway?

Into this darkness Jesus came as a baby, grew to manhood, and announced, "I am the light of the world."[2] He turned on the garage lights of the world that we might see what makes scary sounds in the night. He brought light to the hearts of all men, giving courage and hope, bringing understanding and wisdom that we might live cheerfully.

Of course many men refuse to receive Him. They want nothing to do with a Light that exposes the evil deeds they enjoy, even if it does remove the unknown. But as many as would receive His light, they become the sons of God. To these Jesus said, "Ye are the light of the world."[3] He makes them like cities on hills giving light to travelers for miles around. Through these men God plans to provide direction, relieve fears, give hope, and bring joy to people still sitting in darkness or walking in the night.

When the light of Christ dwells in you, He first shines in your home, whether it's a castle or a tent. Someday you'll be the head of a home, the king. And just as God is the light of heaven you'll have the chance to be the light of your house. When God rules your heart, mind, and actions, you radiate with light. Should you refuse His light in your imagination and deeds, shadows descend upon you and your home.

Ask yourself a simple question, is my heart and home light and cheerful or is it gloomy and sad? The answer reveals whether

---

1. Proverbs 17:27
2. John 8:12
3. Matthew 5:14

you're living a genuine Christian life or an imitation one. You might have chapters of the Bible memorized, attend a church meeting that does everything just so, and be known as a mature young man. Nevertheless, one of the surest tests of a man's religion is this: does he experience joy within and radiate light without? The home of a just man is bright and keeps getting brighter as he walks through life. The house of wicked man is as when the power goes off on a stormy night and everyone fearfully stumbles in the darkness.

If your experience of Christianity is dark and somber, you've missed a turn in the road somewhere and are heading in the wrong direction. The God who created our universe is bright and happy, full of life, and bursting with song. If you always have a gloomy cloud over your head, don't try to fool yourself. God does not have His way in your heart.

If you find yourself in this depressing state, admit it. Cry out as Asaph did when he wrote, "Turn us again, O God of hosts, and cause thy face to shine; and we shall be saved."[1] God is always ready to lighten the man who admits he sits in darkness and genuinely longs for the light.

Even when you have only a little light, you can brighten your world. Anytime you know truth and give it to others, you're spreading light. "Who took my hair brush?" your sister wails, moments before it's time to leave. "I saw it on the shelf in the hall," you quickly reply. You gave light simply by telling the location of her brush. You relieved her fear of going to town with hair looking like a blue jay's nest.

To the discouraged, a man of light speaks words of encouragement. To the angry, he gives reasons to forgive. Wherever he finds darkness, the radiant man pushes it away by speaking and living the truth.

To a tormented friend who wonders what will happen when he dies, a clear presentation of the gospel of Jesus is the greatest display of light ever, and when accepted brightens a heart like the noon-day sun on a ski slope.

Turn over a rotten chunk of wood and you often find termites squirming to avoid tanning their pasty white bodies. They'll hide

---

1. Psalm 80:3

in any dark hole rather than endure the light. Flick on the pantry switch and the cockroaches run for cover like thieves caught in the act. Likewise, evil men run from men of light. By letting God's light dwell in you, those who love darkness scatter. You'll protect your brothers and sisters from troublesome characters because dark-lovers won't want to be around you.

In addition, as moths come to porch lights, you'll attract good young men as friends when you tell the truth, follow the rules, and work hard. These acquaintances will be assets to your family.

I like practical Christianity. It's not just a bunch of ideas to talk about; it's everyday things to do. When you consider bringing light into your home, don't overlook the simple things. Replace light bulbs when they burn out. Wash the windows when you can't see through them. Fix the dome light in the car. When motivated by a desire to bring light to your family, maintenance projects become acts of love rather than boring tasks.

Even something as easy as picking a vase of flowers and setting them on the table adds brightness to any room. It might be just the thing to give your mom a fresh perspective on a particularly trying day.

Life is full of fun and happy things that cheer the hearts of people. Therefore, while you're bringing the truths of the Bible to life in your home, bring in laughter, singing, and the genuine joy of God's presence. It's your privilege.

On a cautionary note, be careful with your light. When you're outside at night, it's no fun to have someone point a flashlight into your eyes from a foot away! Sometimes it even hurts. Similarly, you don't want folks to have to reach for their sunglasses as you make your dazzling appearances. Lasers are beneficial for intricate surgeries. Most of the time, however, useful light is quiet and gentle. Many times a small nightlight plugged into an outlet in the hallway has driven away fear or guided someone safely to the bathroom at midnight. When you brighten lives, be sensitive. Use a dimmer switch on yourself when you need to. Give enough light and truth to be useful, not so much that it blinds.

Many people reject true Light and thereby create dark and fearful places in the world. You don't have to be a part of it. Accept God's offer to shine His light upon you. Then, spread that light, in practical ways, beginning with your family and extending to the ends of the earth.

And they that be wise shall shine as the brightness
of the firmament; and they that turn many to
righteousness as the stars for ever and ever.
(Daniel 12:3)

Questions

- What is a major root of fear?

- How does simple light remove fear?

- Name some ways to bring light into the lives of others.

- How does a man gain the ability to bring light into dark places?

Chapter 19

Sick and Tired of Family Devotions

There is no duty we so underrate as the duty of being happy. By being happy we sow anonymous benefits upon the world.

—Robert Louis Stevenson

It happened many years ago, but it's one of those events a man can never forget. Our family had just finished reading the Bible together at the start of the day. The children ran off to do something in their bedroom. My wife and I stood in the living room. I looked her in the eye and said, "I quit. I'm done. I'm sick and tired of family devotions. I'm not even going to try anymore."

I gave her my reasons. Everyone acted as if it were bedtime. Yawns and slow gazes at the clock punctuated the dull looks. My children showed no signs of interest. Their body language complained of having to sit on the couch and listen to boring statements of biblical content. If anything happened outside the window, they were on their feet in an instant, pointing with excitement, "There's Alphy, the neighbor's dog!" or "It's raining again." I could have given reasons all morning to justify my irritation. My conclusion was: "We are finished."

I didn't mention the real reasons for quitting. She already knew those. I was in a foolish mindset of lashing out at everyone except the real culprit: me. I was tired of boring times together. In my heart I knew the Bible was a living book, but I couldn't present the ideas in a way that seemed interesting to me—let alone to my family. I didn't know how to change. How could these morning meetings be of any use to my children? Was I doing more harm than good? I often boiled inside as I unsuccessfully hid my frustrations.

Doesn't a father have the right to have his family sit pleasantly and listen attentively to his teaching? Shouldn't they be ready to

give enthusiastic answers to his unclear questions and to voluntarily add points of interest to a text he can't explain? I was unprepared and everyone knew it. At one moment, I verbally blamed the trouble on my family, the next moment I inwardly blamed myself. I expected their hearts to be happy, agreeable and spiritually alert, while mine roared with unfulfilled expectations. I couldn't see any way out except to quit. And for a season, that's just what I did.

As you can see, the problem wasn't my family. The problem was me. A statement in Psalm 62:5 describes what my attitude should have been: "My soul wait thou only upon God, for my expectation is from Him." I expected my family to be something I wasn't. I should have been looking to Him—not at them.

As a young man, you may not lead a family yet. Therefore, you might not think this chapter applies to you, but it does. Learn as much as you can about leading a home *before* you have one of your own. Once family life begins, events happen so rapidly that you'll be glad for anything you learned beforehand.

A secret to enjoying family times with God is this: Be a cheerful man who seeks God alone, and then simply invite your family to join you. Let me give you an example.

My friend Paul came into the living room to read his Bible first thing in the morning. Two children sat beside him on the couch, another swept the floor. He began reading a portion of Scripture aloud. One by one, his other six children drifted in, taking seats here and there. At the close of the passage, Paul asked questions for review and to see if his listeners grasped the major points. The seemingly inattentive sweeper responded quickly and accurately. The other children added their insights as well.

There's a place for punctuality. There's a time to sit up straight without moving. There's great value in orderliness. However, there is never an appropriate time for a father to be more interested in the actions and response of his family than in the presence of his God. A happy father, intent upon the person of God, will lead his family further into a personal relationship with Him than an uptight tyrant looking for a perfect performance from his children.

This lesson isn't limited to fathers. Sometimes a Christian pastor or leader is focused on those under his care. If he doesn't concentrate on knowing God himself, and becomes intent only on changing others, that man will end his career frustrated and bitter.

Can you see how this simple lesson carries over into all areas of life? If you, as a young man, learn to cheerfully seek God's presence and go where He tells you to go, you'll be a natural leader. Happily doing what's right usually causes others to want to tag along. It's a secret to being a great daddy should the time come. It's what makes a boss into the man everyone wants to work for. Hopefully it will help you avoid the trap I fell into.

A man cannot successfully lead when he spends more time looking critically upon his followers than happily focusing on the goal ahead.

> *My soul, wait thou only upon God;*
> *for my expectation is from Him.*
> (Psalm 62:5)

Questions

- Why was I frustrated with my family's morning Bible times?

- What was the real problem?

- How will others respond to you if you cheerfully choose a good course of action?

- How old do you have to be before you can apply this lesson?

Chapter 20

Placed in Prison

A little bird I am,
Shut from the fields of air,
And in my cage I sit and sing
To Him who placed me there;
Well pleased a prisoner to be,
Because, my God, it pleaseth Thee.

—Jeanne Guyon

Squawwwk SQUAWWWWK! **SQUAWWWW**WWwww...k. That's chicken language for, "Help! I'm dying!" I ran straight for the pen. When I arrived, all the hens stood looking at me. Not one said a word. After counting beaks numerous times, I concluded: something had happened to one of them.

I investigated the scene. No chicken in the hen house; all nesting boxes rested mysteriously vacant. The inner yard gave no clues either. Upon searching the large fenced area, I found a white fluffy feather lying suspiciously on some sticky brown mud. Toward the corner post was another. On top of the fence perched one more. Occasional feathers trailed toward the creek and out into the woods. My conclusion: Mother Bob Cat had struck again.

She had already snatched sixteen chickens from Glenda's flock, Jonathan's prized goose, and my wife's pet rabbit. She was one smart cat. When we thought the dangers of night were over, we let our animals out of their cages. In the full morning light, she attacked.

For the sake of the remaining hens, I kept them locked in the inner pen where the fencing went over the top and rocks lined the bottom edges. I cooped them up, not because they did anything wrong, but because I wanted to keep them safe. "Into prison you must go, you must go, you must go. Into prison you must go, my fair ladies." They didn't seem to understand what I meant. They didn't like it either. Nevertheless, it was for their good. "Originally, a prison…was only a place of safe custody; but it is now employed as a place of punishment," wrote Noah Webster in 1812.

Most men regard prison as punishment, God usually doesn't.[1] He uses prisons as tools and their keepers as servants to accomplish good works, no matter how cruel the guards might appear. My chickens may have seen me as a malicious slave owner when I was really saving their lives.

Hopefully, none of you are or ever will be in a government jail. Nevertheless, I'm writing as if you are, because we face all kinds of prisons, and the way out is the same for each.

There are two kinds of prisoners. One is taken captive by force. He's overpowered by someone stronger and carried away against his will. By a measure of power or authority he's compelled to lay aside his freedom and obey somebody else's will. If you're in jail, it's probably because you've broken a law. A legal warrant was issued, followed by an arrest, a judgment, and then you were escorted into confinement for a set time. With your freedom restricted, guards watch to ensure that you follow their rules and not your own.

The second type of prisoner is one charmed by beauty. This man voluntarily lets himself be overcome by something pleasing. You've probably seen a foolish boy caught by the beauty of a girl. All he can think about is Miss Cutzie. He blabs on and on

---

1. Matthew 25:46

about her to anyone who'll listen. He awakes thinking about her, eats thinking about her, and cannot concentrate on anything in between because he has willingly let her fill his mind.

Though men let themselves be captivated by many things from Miss Cutzie to robots, cars, dogs, hunting, and more, we were designed to be overcome with the beauty and wonder of the One who created us.

God brings events into your life, removes things and people, and provides adventures that you might be overwhelmed with love and appreciation for Him. By His design you'll always be a prisoner; you have the freedom to choose what type you want to be. Either you're voluntarily captivated by His beauty and excellence, or you're taken prisoner, against your will, by the circumstances and agents God sends for your capture.

What does it mean to be captivated by the beauty of God and how does that keep a man out of prison?

King David said, "One thing have I desired of the Lord, that will I seek after, to behold the beauty of the Lord."[1] To David, the beauty of the Lord was His will, His law, His nature and attributes. David delighted to do that will and enjoyed keeping God's law in his heart.[2] Listen as he expresses his appreciation for God's ways:

> The law of the Lord is perfect, converting the soul:
> The testimony of the Lord is sure, making wise the
>   simple.
> The statutes of the Lord are right, rejoicing the heart:
> The commandment of the Lord is pure, enlightening
>   the eyes.
> The fear of the Lord is clean, enduring for ever:
> The judgments of the Lord are true, and righteous
>   altogether.
> More to be desired are they than gold, yea than much
>   fine gold:
> Sweeter also than honey and the honeycomb.

---

1. Psalm 27:4
2. Psalm 40:8

Moreover by them is thy servant warned:
And in keeping of them there is great reward.[1]

Law is something laid down, like a foundation. It's the rules by which a thing works. The law of gravity holds everything down to the dirt unless some other law, like aerodynamics, takes over. All nature follows laws established at creation. There are laws for societies, for husbands and wives, for what children should do, how to treat people when they fall short, and how to give honor when it's due. All aspects of life and human relationships are governed by laws. All of these laws are part of God's beauty. They are beautiful because they work.

Last week I visited an aviation museum. I had never seen a jet engine before. There was something beautiful about all the tubes and wires surrounding the turbines. The symmetry, order, and complexity were amazing, but the real beauty was that it accomplished the purpose for which it was created. Jet engines push planes, pilots, and passengers all over the sky at tremendous speeds.

God's laws are beautiful because they work. When followed, they lead to peaceful homes, loving relationships, and true joy.

God's beauty is also found in His will. God Himself is the will to do good—at all times and in all places. Mercy, forgiveness, kindness, love, happiness, and endless other wonderful motives continually fill His being. There is nothing else within Him; therefore He must operate from this magnificent perspective. He spanks, reproves, imprisons, and destroys, all with the motives of a good heart, seeking the best for people.

God displays His beauty in creation. When I stand on the edge of a rocky crag looking over a wilderness area, I'm taken in by the beauty of His colors: blue sky, white snow-capped peaks, green forests, gray rocks, black lava fields, and brown cinder cones. At home, that same thrill is available when I touch a wooly caterpillar or observe a dew-covered spider's web.

How can you become captivated by God's beauty when serving a two-year sentence in the state penitentiary?

---

1. Psalm 19:7-11

First, accept the fact that you are where you are by the hand of God. He alone places people in captivity and He alone takes them out. It wasn't the judge, jury, or some false accuser who caused your prison sentence; God designed it and gave it to you for your benefit. Unless you grasp this truth you'll never be free. If you expect some person, agency, or lawyer to get you out, you'll miss the reason for prison. The Lord is your keeper and He'll let you out when He thinks best, not a minute early or a moment late. The apostle Paul never said, "I'm the prisoner of Rome." Instead he frequently declared he was the prisoner of the Lord.[1]

Look for God's beauty in the Bible. Read about what Jesus did and how He treated people. Examine David's thoughts about God in the Psalms. Check out the practical wisdom in Proverbs. The Book explains life and declares the wonder of the Creator. If you can't see God's beauty in His judgments, statutes, and testimonies, it's one reason you've ended up in jail. And, if you won't learn to see His beauty in them, you'll remain in some form of prison all your life.

Appreciate the beauty of His creation. Consider the amazing abilities of a fly, a spider, or a cockroach. How does a fly reverse the lift of his wings when he flips over in flight to land on the ceiling? The light bulb in your cell contains mysteries of science and electricity. Think about it and wonder.

While you're in jail, learn to see God's attributes in people. The crustiest old man has a gem of God's likeness in his nature, a respectable soft spot hiding under the whiskers and scowl. Look for it and you'll find it.

If you want to see something fascinating, you only have to look as far as your hand. Watch as you slowly close your fingers into a fist and open them again. That movement didn't happen by accident. God designed, built, and gave you that hand for good works.

When God sent Israel into captivity by the army of Babylon, He told them to accept their situation, buy land, build houses, raise families, and seek the peace of their prison. In that peace they would find their peace.[2] What can you do to make your

---

1. Ephesians 3:1; 4:1; 2 Timothy 1:8; Philemon 1:9
2. Jeremiah 29

125

prison peaceful? You can't change it all, but what little things can you do? As you attempt to bring quietness and rest to your confinement, you'll gain the wisdom to live at peace when you get out. Instead of pressing your face into the bars pining away for freedom, relax and discover beauty right before your eyes.

If you want to be free from your captivity today, whether it's the state penitentiary, a job to which you feel chained, a home that resembles a jail, or some relationship you're forced to maintain, find your freedom by voluntarily becoming captivated by the goodness of God.

You exist for one purpose: to know and walk with God. Either be captivated by His beauty or be forced into one prison after another. It's your choice.

The reason to get out of jail isn't so that you can do what you want, when you want. The reason to get out is so that you can better fulfill the responsibilities of your situation, whether as a useful son, a faithful husband, or a providing father. If you let your heart become captivated by the wonder of God while in prison, you'll want to perform your responsibilities when you get out. The greatest, most enjoyable, and fulfilling life is that of a man who has the ability to carry out his responsibilities with a heart overcome by the wonder of God. There is no greater freedom.

When you see your prisons as God's plan to stop you from your own ways so that you might consider His beauty, you'll never be confined again.

> **But though He cause grief, yet will He have
> compassion according to the multitude of
> His mercies. For He doth not afflict willingly
> nor grieve the children of men...Let us search
> and try out ways and turn again to the Lord.**
> (Lamentations 3:32-33,40-41)[1]

---

1. related verses: Psalm 79:11; 142:7; Acts 5; 12; 16; Ezekiel 16

Questions

- Was I mean to confine my chickens to a ten-by-twenty-foot pen? Why?

- Why does God put people in prisons?

- How do they get out?

- What does it mean to be captivated by His beauty?

Somewhere around 1685, while imprisoned for her faith, Jeanne Guyon wrote the following poem.

> A little bird I am,
> Shut from the fields of air,
> And in my cage I sit and sing
> To Him who placed me there;
> Well pleased a prisoner to be,
> Because, my God, it pleaseth Thee.
>
> Nought have I else to do.
> I sing the whole day long;
> And He whom most I love to please
> Doth listen to my song;
> He caught and bound my wandering wing;
> But still He bends to hear me sing.
>
> Thou hast an ear to hear
> A heart to love and bless;
> And though my notes were e'er so rude,
> Thou wouldst not hear the less;
> Because Thou knowest as they fall,
> That love, sweet love, inspires them all.
>
> My cage confines me round;
> Abroad I cannot flee;
> But though my wing is closely bound,
> My heart's at liberty;

For prison walls cannot control
The flight, the freedom of the soul.

O it is good to soar
These bolts and bars above!
To Him whose purpose I adore,
Whose providence I love;
And in Thy mighty will to find
The joy, the freedom of the mind.

Chapter 21

Where's the End Zone?

This is and has been the Father's work
from the beginning—to bring us into
the home of His heart.

—George MacDonald

H ave you ever watched a football game where a lineman, in the excitement of recovering a fumble, runs toward the wrong goal? That play becomes the highlight of the game, especially if he makes it to the end zone.

Imagine…the Southerland Salamanders have the ball on their own twenty-yard line. Southerland's fullback takes the handoff from the quarterback and runs up the middle. The linebacker for the opposing Baker City Bullets, knocks the ball out of his hands.

Both teams began diving, sliding, and grabbing for the loose football like the greased pig at the state fair. Unexpectedly the ball bounced off a helmet and into the hands of Clyde Simmons. As a defensive lineman, he had never held a football in a game before. Adrenaline shot through his body. He began running with all his might for the goal.

Unfortunately, Clyde had spun around during the fumble. Instead of running twenty yards to his goal, he began running eighty yards toward the Southerland goal.

When the Southerland fans saw Clyde recover the football, they groaned in dismay. However, when he ran the wrong way, they roared with delight!

The Southerland players almost tackled Clyde before they realized he ran for their goal. Instead of tackling, they formed a wall of blockers escorting him to their end zone.

Clyde Simmons never ran so fast. It was a dream come true, a cheering crowd, an approaching goal line, and a football under his arm.

His teammates were shocked! The linebacker, who had caused the fumble, attempted to tackle Clyde. Southerland blockers kept him from reaching the runaway lineman.

Followed by five Southerland blockers, Clyde entered their end zone. What ecstasy! He dropped the ball and began a victory dance, basking in the roar of the crowd. The alert Southerland players jumped on the football. The officials raised their hands. TOUCHDOWN SOUTHERLAND SALAMANDERS!

Clyde continued to think the crowd cheered for his fabulous fumble recovery, his remarkable run and his tremendous touchdown. Only when the Southerland team began thanking him did Clyde begin to realize his mistake.

Can you imagine the sick feeling that overcame him as his imaginary glory faded away? The fans weren't cheering for him; they jeered at him. Instead of the school hero, he was the school fool! Clyde wished for a place to hide. There was none. He stood in full view of everyone—a lone Bullet in the Southerland end zone.

Many men will come to this same experience when they reach the end of their lives. Thinking they have lived a glorious life, they'll awake to the realization that they had run with all their might to the wrong end of the field. What a devastating realization that will be.

In the Sermon on the Mount, Jesus spoke of many who will run the wrong way. "'Lord, Lord,' they will say, 'have we not

prophesied in thy name? And in thy name have cast out devils? And in thy name done many wonderful works?' And Jesus will say to them, 'I never knew you: depart from me, ye that work iniquity.'"[1] These folks were sure they had reached the goal, but instead found themselves standing at the wrong end of the field.

If these who could prophesy, cast out devils, and do marvelous works got mixed up and ran for the wrong goal, what hope is there for people like you and me? How can we know if we are running in the right direction so that at the end of life we don't hear the words, "I never knew you?"

1. Matthew 7:22 23

God knows that most of us are slow to understand and need things spelled out clearly before we can grasp an idea. Therefore, He makes plain the answers to the most important questions in the universe. He gives clear road signs, marks every turn, and puts flashing lights at life's goal so that all who desire to run there arrive safely. Nevertheless, sometimes the way is so simple that we overlook it.

The goal of life is to delight in God. I wrote it boldly so that you wouldn't miss it. The man who learns to delight in God receives an A on life's final examination. He gets the blue ribbon, the gold medal. And, as he stands in the end zone, his heavenly Father will announce over the loudspeaker, "Well done, good and faithful servant."

We all have the desire and the capacity to experience pleasure. The greatest possible pleasure is to know and enjoy God. If you don't agree, you've probably only known Him from books, meetings, or in activities unrelated to real life. You can know all the facts about God and still miss knowing Him in daily living.

Many men, after tasting sour, godless religion, reject everything they've heard about God. Along with the errors, they throw out the truth. They begin looking elsewhere for something to satisfy their intense, God-given desire for pleasure. Since they have rejected the idea that it could possibly be God, they are like Clyde running away from what they really long for. If Clyde had known where he was going, he would have turned around and risked getting tackled rather than continue to run for the wrong end.

God asks us to love Him with all our heart, soul, mind, and strength, in other words, to delight in Him.

I know a lady who loves chocolate. She doesn't have to eat it to feel pleasure. I've watched her sing about it and lick her fingers in anticipation. Talk about chocolate and she smiles or begins laughing. I'm warning you, don't ever steal her chocolate, nor even pretend to touch it, or you'll see her smile turn into a warning frown. To long for chocolate and then to taste a silky slice is intense pleasure for a chocoholic.

Longing for God with our whole heart, and then receiving the fulfillment of that hunger is an experience that exceeds all pleasures in life. Nothing in this world can compare to it. In addition, when we find our happiness in Him, He is most pleased.

In spite of its simplicity and though the whole Bible declares this truth, many folks still run for the wrong end zone. Some well-meaning people live to preach the gospel, others seek to be missionaries; some find their pleasure in giving money to the poor. All these things are good, but not the goal. You can do them all and be at odds with God at the same time. On the contrary, the man who delights in God cannot help telling the good news. He will give to the poor, but his delight and affection will be to his God; everything else is a sideline.

Some men miss the goal by being good and honest businessmen. They might follow biblical principles and be an example of fine Christian conduct. However, the goal of life is not to be an example of Christian behavior. The goal is delighting in God. The man who delights in God will be a living example of a Christian in business, but his joy will be found in knowing the Creator, not in trying to act like Him.

There's a fine line, but a major difference, between putting on Christian character and letting the happiness of knowing God change your heart. Both may seem the same to someone looking on, but one is a put on, the other is the real thing.

We're all made with an intense desire to know and enjoy our Creator. Nothing but knowing Him, as shown to us in Jesus, will satisfy that longing. We can run all of our lives seeking pleasure in toys, travel, adrenalin rushes, fame, fortune, and relationships, only to miss the true end zone of life, the pleasure of delighting in the One who made us.

The grandstands are full of witnesses watching us run. Will they wince and shake their heads in embarrassment as we scramble for the wrong goal? Or, will they rejoice as they see us reach the true goal of delighting in God?

May you have a heart to run for this end.

Wherefore seeing we also are compassed about with so great a cloud of witnesses, let us lay aside every weight, and the sin which doth so easily beset us, and let us run with patience the race that is set before us. Looking unto Jesus the author and finisher of our faith: who for the joy that was set before Him endured the cross, despising the shame, and is set down at the right hand of the throne of God.

(Hebrews 12:1-2)

Questions

• Why did Clyde Simmons run the wrong way?

• Describe Clyde's feelings when the ball bounced into his hands; as he ran toward the goal; when he entered the end zone; when he realized he was at the wrong end.

• What is the goal of life?

• How can a man run for this goal during a day of work and business?

Chapter 22

McCheyne's Advice

It is a special remedy against fears and sorrows to be much in praise: many a poor, drooping soul hath found it so.

—Matthew Henry

Dad, would you measure me? I want to see if I've grown any."

"I measured you last week, Scott."

"I know. But won't you do it again, just in case I grew a little?"

"Okay," laughed Dad. "Stand up straight. Heels together. Shoulders against the wall. Chin up. Hold still while I mark it. Now, move aside and give me the tape measure. Let's see, five feet...three...annnnd...one-quarter inches."

"Are you sure? That's what I was three months ago! Won't I ever get any taller?"

If Scott quit worrying about his height, ate well, and worked hard, he'd probably grow a few more inches before reaching his maximum stature. And, in the event that five feet, three and one-quarter inches will be his God-given height, he'll save himself the agony of stretching his neck attempting to gain another fraction of an inch.

If we spend too much time calculating and measuring the growth of our body, mind, or spirit, we'll get discouraged. I've watched this trouble especially among men who want to be or do something grand. They are continually measuring their character development or fruitfulness. In both categories they usually find themselves shorter than they wish, resulting in continual frustration. It's hard to live around men who won't accept what they are.

When it comes to practical happiness, a man must understand that he is not the center of the universe. Being overly concerned with personal growth, usefulness and fruit is a well-traveled road to despair. Each honest assessment often reveals new shortcomings rather than positive improvement.

How is it that a man can set out to live a godly life, and after many years still find ugly traits within him? Though his family and friends see a measure or even a remarkable change why does he still get frustrated, and out of sorts?

The Bible takes complicated ideas like these and gives simple answers. The answers sound like fairy tales to the worldly wise, yet they're profoundly true and practically useful. According to the Bible, we've all been bitten by a snake. The poison makes us self-centered and proud. No matter how much reforming we attempt, as long as we live in this body, we'll feel the effects.

When you honestly inspect yourself, hoping to find growth in character or a new measure of spirituality, you'll often find an old problem or some new one stirring up trouble. These discoveries overwhelm and discourage the proud man who seeks self-praise.

There's only one remedy for this poison. When the children of Israel were bitten by snakes, God told Moses to make a bronze serpent and raise it on a pole. Then, when bitten, a man could look up at it and live.[1] This remains the one practical and effective remedy for the despair that plagues self-centered men today.

---

1. Numbers 21:4-9

Eternal life is to know our Father's heart as expressed in Jesus Christ.[1] Therefore, when a man faces despair and discouragement due to his own wickedness, the cure comes by looking to the heart of God.

Relief isn't found in reform and self-discipline. We are warned to work out our own salvation, and that work is simply to look and believe on the good heart of God. Read through the gospels considering Jesus. Study the natural world. Look carefully at history and circumstances. Meditate on God's dealings throughout the Old Testament. All of these show His heart. Look to Him and live.

When faced with the misery of your selfishness, or the discouragement of comparing yourself to the good you see in others, look to the heart of Jesus. Consider His mercy, His understanding, His desire to save sinners, His kindness and His death for you. Instead of piling more guilt upon your head, let your eyes look to your God and be refreshed with hope. Hope, not in your goodness, but in the goodness of the One who loves and saves sinners like you and me.

Communion illustrates this principle. Paul encouraged the Corinthians to examine themselves before taking it. Do you think that after a careful examination they could say, "Oh yes, I'm good enough for communion. I've fasted once a week. I'm not like other men who are unjust and adulterers. I've tithed enough. I've been good." No. Examining ourselves by the candle of the Word usually causes us to say with the publican, "God be merciful to me a sinner."[2]

After seeing ourselves for what we are and confessing our faults, communion leads us to look away from us and soberly consider Him. By eating and drinking we remind ourselves of His broken body and shed blood. It's faith in this blood that lifts the guilt of sin and renews our desire to walk uprightly.

When self-examination reveals our faults, it's useless to crawl on our knees down a path of broken shells or beat our bare backs with a leather strap. Nor is it wise to sulk for an hour in a chair or walk around depressed.

---

1. John 17:3
2. Luke 18:11-14

The biblical response to failure is confessing your faults when you see them, looking to Jesus' heart, and then setting out with hope to do what's right.

Look to Jesus' heart not just when you've done wrong but also when people wrong you. Instead of dwelling on their offense, consider Him. Doesn't He love sinners, isn't He patient with creeps? Even when men were killing Him, didn't He offer forgiveness? The issue isn't those who wrong you, nor is it you, the issue is Him. In knowing Him you find rest and eternal life.

This isn't some form of mental gymnastics; it's how God made us. When we purpose to turn our eyes from ourselves to Him we find freedom from discouragement and the source of genuine joy.

We aren't trying to hide our minds from our failures. With a keen awareness of our faults and the troubles of those around us, we should choose to think about things that are true, honest, just, pure, lovely, of good report, and virtuous.

Ezekiel told the nation of Israel that a day was coming when God would cleanse them from their filthiness and idols; give them a new heart and spirit; put His own spirit upon them so that they would walk in His statutes and judgments; bless them with a land; provide crops and fruitfulness; and *then* they would remember their own evil ways and loathe themselves because of their own iniquities and sins.[1]

You'd think that after being washed, filled, and given a new heart that they would consider themselves good and worthy of praise. That wasn't true for them and it won't be for you. You'll always be needy. The awareness of your need may even grow. Know for sure that God will always be able to meet your need.

On March 20, 1840, Robert Murray McCheyne sent a letter of encouragement to a man including these words, "For one look at yourself, take ten looks at Christ."[2] From time to time, examine yourself, but don't be surprised by the effects of poision you might see. Then, immediately look to the heart of Jesus. Consider His virtue.

---

1. Ezekiel 36:25-31
2. Rev. Andrew Bonar, *Memoir and Remains of the Rev. Robert Murray McCheyne*, (Philadelphia: Presbyterian Board of Publication, 1844), p. 254.

Though you don't want to take your shortcomings and sin lightly, the only remedy for a snake-bitten man is looking to Jesus and getting to know His heart.

Quit measuring yourself, comparing yourself, and accounting the worth of yourself. Turn your eyes upon Jesus, consider Him, and you'll find delight for your soul.

And as Moses lifted up the serpent in the wilderness, even so must the Son of man be lifted up: That whosoever believeth in Him should not perish, but have eternal life.
(John 3:14-15)

Questions

- Why was Scott worried and frustrated?

- Why do people get discouraged when they frequently look at themselves?

- What does it mean to look at Jesus' heart?

- How does looking at His heart give us the freedom to be happy even when we have faults?

- What was Robert Murray McCheyene's advice?

Chapter 23

Two Types of Sorrow

Painful as it may be, a significant emotional event can be the catalyst for choosing a direction that serves us—and those around us—more effectively. Look for the learning.

—Louisa May Alcott

Every finish carpenter makes a mess of sawdust and wood scraps as he goes about his work. Sometimes he has to pick up scraps and sweep more than once a day to safely walk around the job site. Often I'll haul burnable pieces home and throw them into my woodshed for fire starters. One day I decided to take a load from my shed to my brother-in-law, Carle. He heated his house with wood. Surely he could use some kindling.

After loading my truck, I walked back through the house to get my wallet. Passing the empty couch I flopped down, just for a minute, to rest my eyes. I had been working hard lately and it felt good to relax for one minute, or maybe ten. Two hours later I awoke!

Disgusted, I began scolding myself. "You sluggard. You just wasted two good hours of your day. 'A little sleep, a little slumber, a little folding of the hands to sleep…' Poverty is going to run you over. When are you ever going to learn to be diligent?" I had many other unkind words to say to myself as I climbed into the truck and drove down the road. How am I ever going to become the man God wants me to be when I am such a sloth?

With a box of kindling under my arm, I knocked at Carle's door. Within moments he pulled it open. He looked at me, then at the box and exclaimed, "How did you know?"

"How did I know what?" I replied.

"Come in here," he said.

I stepped into the living room. The door of his woodstove stood open. Inside, a wad of paper smoldered between two logs. At that very moment he had been trying to start a fire without kindling. We threw in some fresh paper and a couple of my dry sticks. In no time we had a blazing fire.

As we warmed ourselves, Carle continued to praise God for His timely provision. It wouldn't have been the same if I had arrived two hours before. While driving to his house I kicked myself for being late, but from Carle's perspective I was right on time.

What good is it to rail on yourself when you fall short? Does it make you a better person? Does it help your attitude? Usually it only makes the matter worse while discouraging you and anybody else nearby.

There's a time to be sorry for your failures, for the damage you've caused and the opportunities you've missed. However there are two types of sorrow, one destroys and one leads to life. I expressed the destructive sorrow on the way to Carle's house. If I had shown godly sorrow the incident might have looked something like the following.

"I can hardly believe it! I meant to lie down and rest for ten minutes and it was two hours! What a foolish thing to do. Father, I feel like a failure. I don't want to be a sluggard and yet sometimes I act like one. Will You work in my heart to change me into a diligent worker? Thank You for not giving up on me. Tonight I want to start going to bed earlier so I'll have more energy in the afternoons. Thanks for being merciful to me." Then with a heart of hope, aware of God's goodness, I'd jump in the truck and haul kindling.

Godly sorrow looks right at the problem, confesses it, takes the steps to make it right, and then cheerfully gets back to work. It allows a man to stand clean before God, to be pleasant to people, and be able to look at himself without self-condemnation.

Sorrow is often a pain we feel in our hearts for something we did wrong, or didn't do right. God made us sensitive to an inner pain when we've blown it so we'll change and do something different next time.

In a letter to the Christians in Corinth, Paul describes the proper use of sorrow, "…that ye sorrowed after a godly sort, what carefulness it wrought in you, yea, what clearing of yourselves, yea, what indignation, yea what fear, yea, what vehement desire, yea, what zeal, yea, what revenge! In all things ye have approved yourselves to be clear in this matter."[1] These Corinthians purposed to change their ways. Therefore their sorrow brought life rather than self-destruction.

When you do things you regret, that's not the time to take off your shirt and horsewhip yourself on the back. Instead, it's the time to take a sober look at what happened. When you're wrong, confess it quickly. If you can make it right, begin making it right. If you can see how you should act differently in the future, purpose to change. Godly sorrow sees pain and regret as friends that draw you to the Lord.

Worldly sorrow only weighs a man down. He keeps mentally reviewing his failure, kicking himself and wishing for the chance that will never come to relive the past. He walks through life as if he's carrying a fifty-pound backpack. Instead of dealing with the wrong, paying the price, and walking in freedom, his future is heavy and darkened by a constant focus on past mistakes.

Mistakes can and do hurt. They may cause irreversible consequences. It's the nature of life. That knowledge should give you strong motivation to do what's right. Once you've failed, felt the pain, the regret and the foolishness, instead of choosing the road

---

1. 2 Corinthians 7:11

to a self-condemning prison, let God's sorrow raise you to a new level of manhood. Acknowledge the error, repair what you can, and set your face like a flint to never do it again.

In high school I told a classmate what I thought was a hilarious joke about an epileptic. After telling the story I could hardly stop laughing. She soberly looked me in the eye and said, "I can't laugh at your joke. I have epilepsy." After thirty years I still wince at my thoughtlessness, not because I told it to *her*, but because I told it at all. Once the words came out of my mouth I could not take them back. The damage was done. All I could do was offer a sincere apology and never let it happen again. That incident forever changed my thoughts about jokes.

A man cannot afford to keep looking over his shoulder at his failures, especially if they darken his heart and rob his joy. On the other hand he doesn't want to forget the lessons learned from failures. Godly sorrow frees a man from his past and motivates him to look into the future with hope, confidence, and a measure of humility.

May you find relief and grateful joy as you learn God's reason for sorrow.

> *Now I rejoice, not that ye were made sorry, but that ye sorrowed to repentance: for ye were made sorry after a godly manner...For godly sorrow worketh repentance to salvation...but the sorrow of the world worketh death.*
> (2 Corinthians 7:9-10)

Questions

- In the kindling story, I was concerned with slothfulness. What was God concerned with?

- Describe worldly sorrow. What is its fruit?

- Describe godly sorrow. What happens to the people who have this type of sorrow?

- What pressures will a family face when the father indulges in worldly sorrow?

- What freedoms will a family face when the father uses sorrow as God intended?

Note: This chapter deals with sorrow from failure and sin. Another form of sorrow comes from losing a body part in an accident or not getting the position you worked hard preparing for. Maybe it's having a trusted friend desert you or even the intense pain at the death of a loved one. Though these sorrows are diverse, the principle is the same. Will you see those events through the eyes of worldly sorrow and forever concentrate on something you feel you've lost? Or will you step out of the shadows and look with hope down the new roads these events will lead you. You may always feel a measure of pain. The goal isn't to get away from pain. The goal is to let it work. Let it change your heart. Let it lead you to God.

Chapter 24

An Example to Follow

Most know these things so well as to expect that others should do according to them, but not so well as to do so themselves.

—Matthew Henry

I like reading and enjoy listening. Nevertheless, when it comes to learning a skill like installing an new entrance lock or using a new software program for designing houses, I need somebody to show me how to do it. Reading the instructions helps, but if someone would let me watch them do it just once or twice, I'd be confidently on my way to success.

Jesus' disciples had the same trouble. Therefore, during His last dinner with them, He acted out a most important lesson. Without a lecture or PowerPoint presentation, and with no handouts, He imprinted upon the disciples' minds the road to genuine happiness.

"Knowing that the Father had given all things into His hands, and that He was come from God, and went to God…"[1] Jesus got

---

1. John 13:3

up from the table, tied a towel around His waist, filled a basin with water and began washing His disciples' feet. In just a few hours all these men would deny knowing Him and one in particular would even betray Him. In spite of this, Jesus humbled Himself and, one by one, washed their feet.

When finished, He sat down again and asked, "Know ye what I have done unto you? Ye call me Master and Lord: and ye say well; for so I am. If I then, your Lord and Master, have washed your feet; ye also ought to wash one another's feet. For I have given you an example, that ye should do as I have done to you...If ye know these things, happy are ye if ye do them."[1]

By His example and explanation, Jesus told His disciples that in His kingdom the highest authority stoops to serve the lowest; the richest helps to meet the needs of the poorest; the master provides for the servant; and the purest cleanses the foulest. By actions and words, He drove the lesson home and concluded with a promise that if they would go and do what they had just seen, they'd be truly happy men.

I experienced this happiness early today as I began to write this chapter. My daughters will be driving over the Cascade Mountains to Central Oregon in a few hours. It's been snowing and low temperatures have left the roads covered with ice. Chains or traction tires are required. We have highway tires on the car and therefore they'll need to chain up at some point. That's not a big problem, for the girls know how to install tire chains. The challenge is knowing when to put on chains and when to remove them. It's easy when the snow is everywhere and deep; however when the roads are patched with snow and bare pavement, chains can be more of a problem than a help.

While pausing from writing to stoke the woodstove, my thoughts wandered to the car's tires, installing tire chains, and the black ice predicted before reaching the packed snow. My girls were still sleeping, and even if they had been awake they wouldn't be considering the options and calculating the best courses of action. That's where dads come in.

The thought entered my mind, "Go buy a set of traction tires for the car." The idea came with a burst of joy. Knowing immediately

---

1. John 13:12-15,17

that was the best course of action, I left my sleeping family, jumped into the car, and slowly drove the icy roads to the tire shop. They weren't open yet, but I wanted to be first in line in order to get the tires installed and be home again before departure time.

The girls are now somewhere on the mountain pass as I continue writing to you. The snow outside my window is sparkling like diamonds in the sunlight, but that's nothing compared to the brightness and joy in my heart. It's not the new tires that excite me; it's the privilege of providing them for three girls under my care. It's what a man experiences when he knows what Jesus said and does it.

One reason it's hard for us to understand God's ways is that they're so different from our tendencies. In our minds, the great men should be honored and served and thereby receive pleasure by all the attention and provisions laid at their feet. In God's mind, men experience pleasure by taking the resources within their power and meeting the needs of those under their care. In many godless societies, the weakest and lowest are expected to give what they have in service to the greatest. That's backwards. One recent ruler maintained 170 palaces within his country while some of his people nearly starved. In God's kingdom the strong voluntarily choose to help the weak.

Wrong theories about our natural world tend to turn men away from the truth Jesus lived and taught. Some men proclaim the survival of the fittest has made our natural world what it is today. Adolph Hitler believed so and thereby justified killing people who were, in his eyes, inferior.

The real truth of nature which keeps our world functioning is that the strong lay down their lives for the weak. It's best shown in parents laying down their lives for their young. You'll see it when a rooster attacks an invading raccoon so the hens and chicks might live. It's the mama grizzly taking on anything that comes between her and her roly-poly cub. The life of an emperor penguin egg and chick depends upon a dad who goes without food while balancing it upon his warm feet for nearly five months. Certainly there's a food chain where one animal eats another to live; however, if it were not for the strong parents giving their lives to protect their weaker young, no animals would exist.

The passengers of the Mayflower, those men and women who were the roots of America, understood Jesus' example. They went through terrible hardships, some even to death, that their children might live with the freedom for life, liberty, and the pursuit of happiness. Sure, they wanted their own freedom, but their motivation to come to America came from the desire to provide a place where their children could worship Jesus unhindered.

Lofty ideas aren't worth much until they affect what you do with your hands. So in light of Jesus' lesson that the greater washes the lesser's feet, how are you supposed to act today? Look for somebody weaker. Find somebody who's not as smart as you are, not as rich, not as skilled, or not as observant. Whoever has less than you in anything provides an opportunity for you to act.

Begin at home. Fulfill your primary responsibilities. A father provides for his household or he's worse than an infidel. A son honors his parents. Jesus told His disciples to wait for His promised Spirit and then proclaim the truth first in Jerusalem, their home town and then in Judea, their home country and then unto the uttermost part of the earth.

Begin small. If your little brother wants a drink and he can't reach the faucet, turn it on for him. If your sister can't lift the bag of groceries out of the trunk, help her. As your strength, resources, and skills increase, so will your opportunities to follow Jesus' example and so will your joy. By being faithful in every little chance you get, you'll train your heart to serve your home, your employees and your country when the day comes.

Whether you understood it or not, you've already experienced this happiness. Surely you've provided something for someone less fortunate than yourself. Maybe you've rescued a young friend from the taunts of a bully or carried a bowl of soup to your sister when she had the flu. Happiness comes when you've had the opportunity to share truth with a friend in need of counsel or offered the gospel to a hungry soul. You might even experience a measure of it after removing a tick from your dog's ear.

Jesus' actual example was washing the disciples' feet. Remember His act when one of your family or friends has fallen short. "Brethren, if a man be overtaken in a fault, ye which are spiritual, restore such a one in the spirit of meekness; considering thyself, lest thou also be tempted."[1] If you have an understanding heart, help those who have missed the mark.

Joy comes to the strong when they serve the weak, not because they have done something grand, but because, whether they know it or not, their actions have aligned them with God. He's the happiest Being ever. When you do what He does, you automatically sense His pleasure. It's the way He made you.

"If you know these things, happy are you if you do them."[2]

> *...that which we have seen and heard declare we*
> *unto you, that ye also may have fellowship with*
> *us: and truly our fellowship is with the Father,*

---

1. Galatians 6:1
2. John 13:17

and with his Son Jesus Christ. And these things write we unto you, that your joy may be full.

(1 John 1:3-4)

Questions

• At the last supper, what did Jesus do to teach a lesson?

• What was the lesson?

• If a man knows this lesson, what will make him happy?

• What is something specific you can do to follow Jesus' example?

Chapter 25

Returning

*You may go forth in search of happiness—
but to find it you must return.*

—Timothy Crowley's mother

Wow, there's more to being a building contractor than I ever imagined," replied eleven-year-old Paul. His statement followed my lecture on firm handshakes and looking customers in the eye. When a contractor offers me a limp, fishy handshake and looks away as we meet, I tend to withhold my trust. Instead of starting out on a strong footing, a slight sense of suspicion creeps into my mind.

Handshakes and straight-on looks are a small part of construction; many would-be carpenters have never given them a thought. Neither have they considered being punctual, wiping their feet before entering a kitchen remodel, billing promptly, wearing appropriate clothing, or even brushing their teeth. Though not related to cutting lumber and nailing on trim, these little things are important in the minds of current and future clients.

Likewise, there are aspects of practical happiness most folks never consider. One, is a heart skilled in returning. At first thought this may hardly make sense, but hopefully in a few minutes you'll understand the beauty, wisdom, and joy of possessing a returnable spirit.

Most of us tend to run from difficult or uncomfortable situations. If you get in a driving accident, your first impulse may be to run before inquiring whether anyone is hurt. If you run, and are caught, you'll face serious fines and possibly imprisonment.

Suppose a bike rider darts out of an alley, and you run over him with your car. In America, if you return to give him aid, even if he should die, you'll suffer no punishment. If you drive away in fear, you'll probably go to jail for killing him when you're caught. Hit-and-run laws are on the books because people have a tendency to run from their problems and responsibilities.

A clothing store clerk makes a mistake, overcharges, or acts rudely. "I'll never go back to that store as long as I live," announces the upset customer. And many times, he doesn't. He mentally builds a fence around the place and avoids it. When the grocer offends him, that customer won't go there either; next it's the florist, the gas station attendant, the waiter, and on and on. After cutting off all the local businesses through unresolved conflicts, the displeased customer may need a new car to drive across town to shop.

A man with a heart unwilling to return and restore broken relationships may very well end up divorcing his wife and adding her name to his black list along with her friends and relations. Then he may take up an offense with a church and avoid everyone who ever attended the congregation. If he never returns to the messes and misunderstandings he's neglected, eventually he'll have so many people to avoid that he'll need to move to another town to start over.

You can't live a happy life when you leave unresolved quarrels behind you. By refusing to think about the past, a man might find some measure of comfort. However, our minds will occasionally replay our lives whether we like it or not. If we've ignored our messes, every review brings a little sadness that keeps us from resting in joy.

When somebody wrongs you, go to him. Tell him his error. Create an opportunity to make things right.[1] Don't just sulk in your corner waiting for him to figure out what's wrong. Go back. Unless you do, you might lose some precious things like a friend, a good name, and a measure of happiness.

When you've wronged somebody, return. To the best of your ability, make it right.[2] No matter who's at fault, it's your responsibility to go back.

Work at every job in such a way that on the last day the boss will say, "If you need work in the future, come back. You'll always have a job." Even when you never plan to return, leave all the doors open behind you. You never know what good might catch up to you through the open doors you've left behind. You'll find answers to the question, "What am I going to do with my life?" more often by looking at the familiar doors behind you than knocking on new ones down the hall.

Some folks "burn bridges" while traveling through life. That means they say and do things that ruin relationships and then never go back and repair them. It's a foolish way to live.

Returning has tremendous potential. Doesn't it make you happy when you restore a broken friendship, when you've gone back and completely finished a job, or when you've returned a borrowed tool? Even a crook finds relief when he turns himself in.

Returning isn't just to fix wrongs, it can underline good. After ten lepers were healed, only one returned to give thanks.[3] Instead of heading off to the next adventure, it's worth our while to go back and thank people, reminding them of our appreciation and gratitude.

When we consider returning to repair a wrong, or in some cases to do something good, we tend to face lies that hinder us, "They won't want to see you. You'll look stupid. It won't do any good. You'll make things worse." If we listen, those lies become fences, keeping us from the happiness that's waiting for those who return. Maybe someone will reject your efforts to right a wrong, but most won't; God never will. He's always ready to welcome

---

1. Luke 17:3
2. Matthew 5:23-24
3. See their story in Luke 17:11-19.

your wholehearted return, though the lies scream loudest against Him.

Developing a returning spirit in all areas of life, from library books to crimes, helps fit a man for the most important return he'll ever face. "All we like sheep have gone astray; we have turned every one to his own way."[1] At some point, every man must return to God. For without returning from our ways to His, there's no hope of any future happiness.

Hear what God has to say on the matter, "I have blotted out, as a thick cloud, thy transgressions, and as a cloud, thy sins: return unto Me; for I have redeemed thee."[2] He's cleared the road that leads to Him, should we ever choose to take it. "Have I any pleasure at all that the wicked should die? Saith the Lord God: and not that he should return from his ways and live?"[3]

Jesus told one of the best return stories ever. It's the one about a prodigal son. The boy had done wrong and ended up in a far away country. He became so hungry that he wanted to eat pig's slop. Finally, "When he came to himself, he said, How many hired servants of my father's have bread enough and to spare, and I perish with hunger! I will arise and go to my father, and will say unto him, Father, I have sinned against heaven, and before thee, and am no more worthy to be called thy son: make me as one of thy hired servants. And he arose, and came to his father. But when he was yet a great way off, his father saw him, and had compassion, and ran, and fell on his neck, and kissed him. And the son said unto him, Father, I have sinned against heaven, and in thy sight, and am no more worthy to be called thy son. But the father said to his servants, Bring forth the best robe, and put it on him; and put a ring on his hand, and shoes on his feet: And bring hither the fatted calf, and kill it, and let us eat, and be merry: For this my son was dead, and is alive again: he was lost and is found. And they began to be merry."[4]

The son had no idea his return could be so joyful. He had been listening to the same lies that keep you and me from

---

1. Isaiah 53:6
2. Isaiah 44:22
3. Ezekiel 18:23
4. Luke 15:17-24

returning to acknowledge our failures. If he had known the truth, wouldn't he have come home sooner?

As you consider returning to God, whether it's over a small matter, or maybe like the prodigal son, you want to turn your whole life back to Him, remember: there's a party, beyond your wildest imagination, waiting for you. Disregard the lies and return to the Shepherd and Bishop of your soul. There's no happier place in the world.

In returning and rest shall ye be saved.
(Isaiah 30:15)

Questions

- What does a firm handshake have to do with carpentry?

- What is a hit-and-run accident?

- What happens to men who will never go back to make things right?

- What is the most important return we'll ever make?

- What will try to keep you from returning to what you know is right?

- If a young man is an overcomer, how will he treat these obstacles?

- Do you have someone in mind you need to return to?

As I finished the first draft of this chapter, I convicted myself. Years ago a lumber company made an accounting mistake. It cost me a couple hundred dollars. When the owner couldn't see the problem, I responded like a fool, gave up on him, and went somewhere else for my lumber. Before continuing to write this chapter, I need to return and set that relationship right. It makes me nervous to think about it. With the snow falling I have a good excuse to stay home; however, I don't want to miss the party. I must confess, I don't feel like it's going to be a happy party; the lies are getting to me. Nevertheless, if I'm going to encourage you to return, I have to do so myself. I'll let you know how it goes.

Later...

The owner sat in his office surrounded by stacks of papers. He greeted me with, what seemed to be, a slight hesitancy. He may have sensed the same in me. I reminded him that we had had a disagreement years back and confessed that my response to our difference was worse than the issue itself. I told him I was wrong and wanted to make it right. We chatted warmly for a few minutes, philosophized about life, and gave our opinions about the current business environment. He told me that my account has always been open and that if there was anything he could do to help in the future, he'd gladly assist me.

We parted as two old friends. I think our relationship is warmer than it ever has been in the past.

Why did I take so long to go back? It was those lies: "You don't need to do it. It was so long ago. He'll think you're stupid. It won't make any difference. It was his problem not yours." You'd think at my age, and with all the return trips I've had to make, it would get easier. I should have seen through the curtain of lies that blocked my road to the party, but I never completely can. They hounded me all the way to the owner's office, and never left until I shook his hand and looked him in the eye. The happiness that followed this, and every return trip, is worth far more than the struggle it takes to get me there.

May you have the courage to do what you know is right and get back in time for the party.

Chapter 26

Produce Fruit

God is going to reveal to us things He never revealed before if we put our hands in His. No books ever go into my laboratory. The thing I am to do and the way of doing it are revealed to me. I never have to grope for methods. The method is revealed to me the moment I am inspired to create something new. Without God to draw aside the curtain I would be helpless.

—George Washington Carver

While eating a continental breakfast in the lobby of a motel, my family and I couldn't help hearing the television station bellowing above the room full of chatting travelers. The news station broadcasted an interview with America's First Lady, Laura Bush.

"Are you happy?" the announcer questioned.

"Yes, I am very happy," returned Mrs. Bush. "If you are doing what you love and feel productive, whether at home or on a job, you're happy."

The president's wife understood one secret of happiness: accomplish something useful. The varying moods of a hive of honeybees illustrate this same principle.

If you're interested in honeybees, and want your first experience opening a hive to be pleasant, chose sometime around noon on a warm late spring or early summer day to remove the top cover. Experienced beekeepers successfully inspect their hives year-round. Nevertheless, on your first attempt, I'd recommend a warm day when blooms abound.

In the middle of a summer day, most of the foraging bees are out visiting flowers. Those in the hive have returned with full tanks of nectar. The interior workers are busy cleaning cells, building comb, and caring for all the other duties of a colony. Even the guards at the entrance seem to be relaxed as load after load of sweet juice enters their checkpoint. At such a time, when you lift the cover from the hive you hear a quiet hum of pleasant activity. They usually don't mind a gentle dismantling of the entire hive as long as they can keep working.

In contrast, try pulling the lid off a hive on a chilly day in the fall when few plants are blooming. As you slide your hive tool under the lid and carefully break their propolis seal, your ears may detect a low growl, almost like a dog's first warning to keep away from his food. Peeking in, you might see the top frames covered with an army of bees standing at attention, stingers slightly raised as if to say, come ahead, make our day. Without profitable work, the whole hive seems at odds and looks for anything moving as a target for their frustrations. An idle hive is a fighting hive.

People are similar. They'll complain about work as if it's a wicked curse. However, I've never seen a genuinely happy lazy person. They claim to have the best of lives lounging around eating candy and playing video games, but don't believe them. Superficially, their limited experience may seem great, but idle people feel sort of sick most of the time. If they tell you otherwise, it's only because they've never felt the freedom and health of hard work. They don't have a clue about the happiness diligent folks enjoy.

Unproductive people tend to get into trouble. I don't know who came up with the phrase, "Idle hands are the devil's workshop," but whoever it was didn't imagine the idea in a moment of contemplation. He realized it by watching the results of empty lives wandering into places they didn't belong. When not about their own business, people often become busybodies meddling in other's affairs.

The church at Thessalonica believed Jesus was coming back soon. Some of them quit useful employment and idly waited for the approaching day. Problems began developing, and for this reason the apostle Paul wrote a warning.

In the letter he said, "Withdraw yourselves from every brother that walketh disorderly, and not after the tradition which he received of us. For yourselves know how ye ought to follow us: for we behaved not ourselves disorderly among you; neither did we eat any man's bread for nought; but wrought with labor and travail night and day, that we might not be chargeable to any of you: not because we have not power, but to make ourselves an example unto you to follow us. For we hear that there are some which walk among you disorderly, working not at, but are busybodies. Now them that are such we command and exhort by our Lord Jesus Christ, that with quietness they work, and eat their own bread. But ye, brethren, be not weary in well doing."[1]

Quietly work, provide at least enough for food, and do well. That's sound advice from two perspectives. First, your needs are met and you're not a burden on others. Second, by working for basic needs you don't have time to entangle yourself in your neighbor's superficial troubles. These simple rules lead to practical happiness that officious people often forfeit.

I try not to use big words; however, "officious" is a good one to learn. It describes a man excessively zealous to serve, interposing in affairs without being desired. He thinks he's the hero with the answers instead of the troublesome nuisance others perceive him to be.

On a stroll through the city park, Sam sees a bunch of guys playing basketball on the playground. Their intensity and skill attract his attention. He stops to watch. A forward for the red shirts elbows the blue shirts' center. The blue shirts' guard travels with the ball and gets away with it. Numerous other infractions take place as the two teams battle it out. Sam's been a referee at the local middle school for two years, and with an air of knowing some rules, runs onto the court. The next time the forward elbows the center, Sam blows the whistle he keeps around his neck, juts out his arm at the forward and yells, "Foul!" Twenty tennis shoes skid to a stop, ten faces with dropped-jawed unbelief turn his way, and one loud mouth says, "Where did you come from. Get off the court before we throw you off!" Lowering his ears below his shoulder blades, Sam makes a hasty retreat, not only off the court, but out of the park! He saw himself as a referee or an official. In reality he was "officious."

If Sam had been busy with his own responsibilities, like working for his food, he wouldn't have gotten into trouble. His free time allowed him to get involved where he didn't belong.

---

1. 2 Thessalonians 3:6-13

Those teams liked playing their style of basketball and it was none of Sam's business interfering.

Often folks with excessive free time talk and hear too much. After listening to a measure of gossip, they set out to cure Martha's marriage troubles, discipline Darren's children, or educate Elmer on his need for personal hygiene. Each of these folks may need some help. Nevertheless, getting involved where a man doesn't belong is one path to an unhappy and troublesome life. Stay away by quietly doing your own work.

That doesn't mean you won't help people. Remember, Paul finished his warning against busybodies with, "Be not weary in well doing." There's a balance. Attend to your responsibilities, save up resources, and when invited or commanded by an authority, help everyone you can.

Productive work produces happiness. It doesn't merely avoid trouble; it's a foundational reason for our existence. On the night before Jesus died, He taught many lessons. Most dealt with the future happiness and present comfort of His disciples. In one parable about the vine and the vinedresser, He said, "I am the vine and my Father is the husbandman, Every branch in me that beareth not fruit he taketh away: and every branch that beareth fruit, he purgeth it, that it may bring forth more fruit…I am the vine, ye are the branches: He that abideth in me, and I in him, the same bringeth forth much fruit: for without me ye can do nothing…Herein is my Father glorified, that ye bear much fruit; so shall ye be my disciples…These things have I spoken unto you, that my joy might remain in you, and that your joy might be full."[1]

God looks for fruit. He's given us everything we need to produce it. His care and pruning prepare us for a maximum crop. As we abide in Him, His life within us will produce fruit in its seasons and we'll nearly burst at the seams with joy.

From experience, Mrs. Bush knew productive work made her happy. The Bible tells us why. Fruitful work aligns us with God and His joy. Therefore, the diligent tend to know a happiness the lazy cannot imagine.

---

1. John 15:1 and following

*In all labor there is profit: but the talk of the
lips tendeth only to penury [extreme poverty].*

(Proverbs 14:23)

Questions

- Why are bees usually happy on warm days?

- What were the Thessalonians doing that made Paul write what he did?

- What does *officious* mean?

- Why does productive work tend to make a man happy?

Chapter 27

Pain, the Preacher

In the modern view pain is an enemy, a sinister invader that must be expelled. And if Product X removes pain thirty seconds faster, all the better. This approach has a crucial, dangerous flaw: once regarded as an enemy, not a warning signal, pain loses its power to instruct. Silencing pain without considering its message is like disconnecting a ringing fire alarm to avoid receiving bad news. Pain is no invading enemy, but a loyal messenger dispatched by my own body to alert me to some danger.

—Dr. Paul Brand

One winter morning, I began installing blocks between the second-floor joists on the house we were framing. My fingers felt like icicles dangling from my knuckles. Somehow, I laid my left thumb on one of those blocks without telling my right hand what I'd done. With the full swing of a 32-ounce, waffle-faced hammer, instead of driving the block into place, I pulverized my thumb.

YyyyyyyeeeeeeeeeeeeooooooooooooooooouuuuuuuuuuuCH!

Shortly after I started framing houses, my left hand was a mess. Gauze and tape wrapped a swollen thumb, a metal splint protected the wounds on my pointer finger, and another round of gauze and tape covered the middle finger. I set nails for my oversized hammer between my bandaged middle finger and a nervous ring finger. Though strongly motivated, I couldn't always control my hammer. Nevertheless, I learned a valuable lesson about controlling pain's intensity.

Whenever I smashed a finger, dropped a beam on my toe, or executed any one of hundreds of other pain-producing stunts a carpenter might devise, I paused and thanked God for the body parts that still worked. "Thank You God, I can still bend my little finger; thank You I can walk." It amazed me how a simple expression of gratitude drastically cut my sense of pain. It was like grabbing the volume control on a loud radio and turning it down.

Years after discovering this pain reliever, I couldn't walk due to a back injury. While lying on the couch thanking God for my arms and my neck, my daughter loaned me a fascinating book, *The Gift of Pain* by Phillip Yancey and Dr. Paul Brand.

One clinical study concluded that "gratitude is the single response most nourishing to health."[1] What I had learned from the job site had been proven in a clinic! Dr. Brand also observed that the emotions of fear, anger, guilt, loneliness, and the feeling of helplessness increase a person's sensitivity to pain. A needle-fearing patient tends to hurt more from a doctor's shot than a relaxed recipient.

Though gratefulness for my healthy parts proved a useful step in curbing construction pains, I had more to learn. It had never occurred to me to thank God for the actual pain! Brand's book helped me to understand that pain itself is good and wise.[2]

One way to increase your appreciation for pain is to consider life without it. At first it sounds great; however, when you realize the truth, life without pain is horrifying. A child without the sensation of pain might accidentally cut off the tip of his finger or step on a nail and keep walking without even a limp until his whole foot is swollen and red with infection. Without pain he might leave his hand on a red hot stove, unaware that it's burning through his skin. These examples are terrible and I'd rather not think about them. Nevertheless, I wrote them because

---

1. Philip Yancey and Dr. Paul Brand, *The Gift of Pain* (Grand Rapids, MI: Zondervan Publishing House, 1993), p. 222.

2. Ibid., p. 223.

I don't want you to ever forget that God mercifully and with great kindness gave us the ability to hurt. Pain is a friend. You cannot imagine the misery of living without it.

Pain pushes us from self-destruction and steers us toward God like a well-trained Border collie herds sheep. Understand pain's purpose and you gain a measure of freedom to face afflictions with calmness. You may still hurt, but pain becomes a welcome companion instead of an enemy you scream to avoid.

Amos, an Old Testament prophet, described God's use of pain, "I have given you cleanness of teeth and want of bread... yet you have not returned unto me, saith the Lord. I have withholden the rain from you...yet ye have not returned unto me...I have sent among you the pestilence after the manner of Egypt: your young men have I slain with the sword, and have taken away your horses; and I have made the stink of your camps to come up unto your nostrils: yet have ye not returned unto me, saith the Lord...prepare to meet your God, O Israel."[1]

Amos warned Israel that if they refused pain's prompting to return from their wicked ways, God would increase it until the pain became everlasting. God uses pain to motivate men because it's usually what humans obey most. For a man to successfully resist God his whole life, he must endure much unnecessary pain; for God will often increase the volume to get a wayward man's attention.

Dr. Brand wrote, "Think of pain as a speech your body is delivering about a subject of vital importance to you...From the very first twinge, pause and listen to the pain and, yes, try to be grateful. The body is using the language of pain because that's the most effective way to get your attention. I call this approach 'befriending' pain: to take what is ordinarily seen as an enemy and to disarm and then welcome it."[2]

Pain is often a dear friend telling us there's a different way to live than what we've chosen or that something is wrong and needs attention. It can be anything from a mosquito biting our arm to the ache in our hearts when we're at odds with a friend.

---

1. Amos 4:6-12
2. Yancey and Brand, p. 222.

I meet many men who experience chest pains. The pressures of jobs and home become too much for their nerves. Their chests tighten and begin hurting. Many turn to pain-relieving pills or drinking at a tavern on the way home. Pain is the messenger pleading with them to slow down and change perspective or directions. Without stopping to ask, "Why do I hurt?" they'll often find something to numb the pain enough to stay on their misguided course.

I want you to be aware of these things while you're young, so that you might be alert as you get older. Maybe you could change your ways before tension turns into a heart attack or a nervous breakdown. In addition, I want you to know it so you might have mercy and compassion on men who seek help from drugs or alcohol. You can't blame a man who has never heard the gospel, or one who refuses to believe, from trying to stop his pain any way possible. Sadly, his cover-up attempt will, at best, be a temporary fix.

Sometimes we experience pain by no fault of our own: another driver runs into our car, a terrorist throws a bomb; maybe we have a genetic disease or pain for which there's no explanation. One thing we can be sure of, if we let the pain turn our eyes toward God, it won't be wasted.

For those with unexplained injuries, illnesses, or for those enduring torture for their faith, be assured: pain only exists under God's control. He sets the limits, never gives more than we can bear, and for the Christian, it's temporary. There's a day coming when it will end.

Sometimes God completely shields a man from pain. Consider Stephen. When stoned, he didn't focus on the rocks, but on his God. He knelt, prayed that God would forgive his killers, and went to sleep.[1] Many times in emergencies, people with serious injuries never feel them until they've completed their responsibilities or rescued someone from serious danger. It's part of God's wise use of pain.

Woe to those who don't listen when pain speaks, "And the fifth angel poured out his vial upon the...beast; and his kingdom

---

1. Acts 7:59-60

was full of darkness; and they gnawed their tongues for pain, and blasphemed the God of heaven because of their pains and their sores, and repented not of their deeds."[1] "And the Devil that deceived them was cast into the lake of fire and brimstone, where the beast and the false prophet are, and shall be tormented day and night for ever and ever."[2]

This won't happen to those who turn to God. On the last day of this world, pain's preaching and compelling stops. For those who repented, "...God shall wipe away all tears from their eyes; and there shall be no more death, neither sorrow, nor crying, neither shall there be any more pain...."[3]

Until that day, be thankful for your gift of pain. Don't waste it. Let pain be a friend and preacher who draws you to God.

Is any among you afflicted? Let him pray.
(James 5:13)

Questions

- Name one attitude that relieves pain.

- What are five emotions that tend to increase pain?

- Can you think of five opposite emotions that might reduce pain?

- What are a couple of reasons why God gives us pain?

- When there's pain that you don't understand or when you may be tortured for your faith, what are three comforting facts to remember?

1. Revelation 16:10-11
2. Revelation 20:10
3. Revelation 21:4

Chapter 28

Persecution

...but by the simple power of truth; we witness
a soul so under the influence of good, that
evil, even in its most cruel form, cannot dim its
beauty, but serves as a contrast to heighten its
luster...for it is in the arena, at the stake, and
in the dungeon that the religion of Christ has
won its most glorious triumphs.

—Introduction to *Foxe's Book of Martyrs*

It always thrills me to catch a glimpse of God's wisdom. His perspective is not limited to this world. He understands how all knowledge and experience connects, not just on earth but in the world to come. Nothing is a mystery to Him. Just when we think we have something figured out, He brings in new facts that show we've hardly scratched the surface of His understanding.

Therefore, when it comes to grasping practical happiness, we must go to the highest possible viewpoint in an attempt to gain God's perspective of the matter.

Jesus said, "Blessed are they which are persecuted for righteousness' sake: for theirs is the kingdom of heaven. Blessed are ye, when men shall revile you, and persecute you, and shall say all manner of evil against you falsely, for my sake. Rejoice, and be exceeding glad: for great is your reward in heaven: for so persecuted they the prophets which were before you."[1]

Jesus could not have said this without confidence that life is more than the world we see. He endured the cross for the joy that was set before Him. He saw something beyond pain and death. That vision gave Him a delight that scourging, crucifixion, and bearing the world's sin couldn't darken.

We need this same vision to maintain happiness in troubled times. Once you grasp it, nothing can steal your joy. Not only can no one steal it, their very attempts may cause rejoicing beyond what we have ever experienced or imagined.

It's an amazing design that brings exceeding gladness through fiery trials. That's why Isaiah proclaims that God's ways are higher than our ways. If the very worst, cruelest, and meanest things men can do to you produce the highest joy, what do you have to fear?

When Jesus said, "...the Son of man must suffer many things, and be rejected of the elders, and of the chief priests, and scribes, and be killed...Peter took him, and began to rebuke him."[2] Jesus responded by telling Peter that he valued the things of this world more than the things of God.

About thirty years later, Peter had grown in his perspective of God. He encouraged fellow believers by writing, "But and if ye suffer for righteousness' sake, happy are ye: and be not afraid of their terror, neither be troubled...Beloved, think it not strange concerning the fiery trial which is to try you, as though some strange thing happened unto you: But rejoice, inasmuch as ye are partakers of Christ's sufferings; that, when His glory shall be revealed, ye may be glad also with exceeding joy."[3]

Not only did Peter write about his change of heart, he lived it. After nine months in prison, Nero ordered him scourged and crucified. After the scourging, he requested to be crucified head down. Peter could mock his own death because he saw God's kingdom coming.

Foxe's Book of Martyrs recounts God's goodness toward men and women enduring persecution. Story after story tell of how

1. Matthew 5:10-12
2. Mark 8:31-32
3. 1 Peter 3:14; 4:12-13

He allowed them insight into the future kingdom, giving them confidence and delight. Revealing His presence brought them courage to face evil attacks with calmness and even radiant joy. The following is one example:

> William Hunter had been trained to the doctrines of the Reformation from his earliest youth, being descended from pious parents, who carefully instructed him in the principles of true religion…One day, finding the chapel open, he entered, and began to read in the English Bible, which lay upon the desk, but was severely reprimanded by an officer of the bishop's court, who said to him, "William, why meddlest thou with the Bible? Understandest thou what thou readest? Canst thou expound Scripture?" He replied, "I presume not to expound Scripture; but finding the Bible here, I read for my comfort and edification." The officer then informed a priest…the priest severely chided him, saying, "Who gave thee leave to read the Bible?" …And on telling him…not to meddle with the Scriptures, [William] frankly declared his resolution to read them as long as he lived, as well as reproved the vicar for discouraging persons from that practice, which the Scriptures so strongly enjoined. The priest then upbraided him as a heretic…
>
> After two days the bishop sent for him, and demanded whether he would recant or not. But William made answer that he would never recant that which he had confessed before men as concerning his faith in Christ…The Bishop then sent him to the convict prison, and commanded the keeper to lay as many irons upon him as he could bear; and moreover, asked him how old he was.
>
> William said that he was nineteen years of age. "Well," said the bishop, "you will be burned before you be twenty, if you will not yield yourself better than you have done yet."
>
> He now continued in prison three quarters of a year during which time he was taken before the bishop five times. The bishop…reasoned with him saying, "If thou

wilt yet recant, I will make thee a free man in the city, and give thee forty pounds in good money to set thee up in thine occupation; or I will make thee steward of my house, and set thee in office."

"I thank you for your great offers," answered William; "But notwithstanding, my lord, if you cannot persuade my conscience with Scriptures, I cannot find in my heart to turn from God for the love of the world; for I count all worldly things but loss and dung in respect to the love of Christ."

William's father and mother came to him…and desired heartily of God that he might continue to the end as he had begun, and his mother said to him that she was happy to have such a child, who could find in his heart to lose his life for Christ's sake.

William said to his mother, "For the little pain I shall suffer, which will soon be at an end, Christ hath promised me, mother, a crown of joy; should you not be glad of that?"

Whereupon his mother kneeled down on her knees, saying, "I pray God strengthen thee, my son to the end; yea, I think thee as well bestowed as any child I ever bore."

Next morning, Mr. Brocket, the sheriff, called to bid him prepare for his fate. At the same time the son of Mr. Brocket came to embrace him, saying, "William, be not afraid of these men with bows, bills, and weapons ready prepared to bring you to the place where you shall be burned."

"I thank God I am not afraid," replied the undaunted youth, "for I have reckoned what it will cost me already." …Then said the sheriff, "Here is a letter from the queen; if thou wilt recant, thou shalt live; if not, thou shalt be burned."

"No," said William; "I will not recant, God willing." He then rose up and went to the stake, and stood upright against it…He then prayed, "Son of God, shine upon me!" and immediately the sun in the heavens shone out of a dark cloud so full in his face, that he was constrained to look another way; whereat the people wondered, because it was so dark a little time before.

William then cast his psalter into his brother's hand, who said, "William, think on the holy passion of Christ, and be not afraid of death."

"I am not afraid," answered William. Then lifting up his hands to heaven, he said "Lord, Lord, Lord, receive my spirit!" and...yielded up his life for the truth. March 27, 1555, England.[1]

Mr. and Mrs. Hunter had trained their son in this mysterious way of God: the foundation of true joy rests beyond the edges of this world. Jesus, Peter, and William lived as men who knew it.

Life's events, especially those that are unjust and cruel, will steal your joy if your hopes are based here. By God's grace, may you be a man like William Hunter, so confident of the coming joy that nothing can take it away.

Therefore work hard with your hands, be a good citizen, and fix your mind on the Kingdom to come and upon the happy King who rules it all.

> ***Wherefore let them that suffer according to the will of God commit the keeping of their souls to Him in well doing, as unto a faithful Creator.***
> (1 Peter 4:19)

Questions

• Why could Jesus be joyful as He approached the cross?

• How does a man develop the eyes to see into God's coming kingdom?

---

1. John Foxe, *Foxe's Book of Martyrs,* (Old Tappan, NJ: Fleming H. Revell Company, 1968), pp. 231-236.

- What did William's parents think about his upcoming death?

- Was William afraid?

- How is it possible that cruel tortures cause rejoicing in Christians?

Chapter 29

Outwitting a Weak Mind

The mind is its own place, and in itself can make
a heav'n of hell and a hell of heaven.

—John Milton, *Paradise Lost*

Through the years, most of my writing has been done while my family sleeps. Usually it's before they get up in the morning and prior to my heading off to work. It can take weeks to complete an idea to the point where an editor can take over.

This month I tried something new. I decided to not accept any building jobs, but to write every day until I finished the project, ran out of money, or out of mind, whichever came first. It was startling, though not amazing, that I ran out of mind the night before I began!

I planned to start Tuesday morning. On Monday night, what began as a pleasant interaction turned into a family discussion that left everyone in tears, especially me. At the end I felt like a complete failure as the leader of our home.

After praying together, everyone went to bed, except for me. I went downstairs to my woodshop, stoked up the fire, grabbed a folding chair, sat down and stared into the flames. I told God of my shortcomings and asked for help. My mind ran in circles, blaming myself for not being the dad I could have or should have been. I wondered what to do and sometimes my mind seemed to go blank.

Back in my college years I would occasionally sit all day, unable to focus on what to do next, lost in discouragement. Sometimes a dark cloud hung over my head for weeks. This wasn't college days. I had a family to protect and provide for. I couldn't afford to spend even one hour lost in some form of depression. I had to quit staring into the fire.

I don't know the names for mental troubles. I just know I have a weak mind that doesn't always work the way I want it to. It's frail, sensitive and easily discouraged. I've had to learn to outwit it.

Hopefully, your mind is a little more stable. Nevertheless, I want to tell you of one lesson that I've learned, by experience, which gets me through the dark days, when it seems I've lost my way.

It's called responsibility. Someone walks into the room and says hello. If you respond, you'll say hello in return. Respond means to send back. Any polite person feels obligated to send back a reply when spoken to. A man who consistently replies to life's hellos or its obligations is called responsible.

In the emergency world, a first responder replies quickly when called for help. Ambulance drivers and firemen trained in medical and rescue skills are first responders. They offer their lifesaving talents at a moment's notice. When someone calls, "Hello, I need help," they answer by sending themselves. A fireman may feel sad, lonely, or even depressed; however, when the bell rings, he immediately jumps into his turnouts and runs for the truck, answering his responsibilities.

One way to outwit a weak mind is by simply replying to your obligations. If you ever feel like you can't think straight, take a shower, brush your teeth, and use some of that deodorant your aunt gave you for your birthday. If it's your turn to wash the dishes, wash 'em. If you need to apologize to your brother, don't put it off. Button your shirt. Put your dirty laundry in the hamper. Hang up your coat. Even if they are just little things, reply to your obligations. Do as many simple and responsible acts as your weak mind can handle.

When my sister's husband died, there were days when she could hardly keep going. We had a saying between us, "Keep your shoes tied." That meant, do the little things you know you need to do, the ones you *can* do; you'll get through.

Back to my discouraging evening: Though the fire seemed to hold my gaze like an electromagnet, I knew I must not keep looking at it. Out of the corner of my eye, I noticed the empty wood box next to the stove. Breaking my stare, I went to the woodshed, cut a load of kindling and filled the box. Looking through tears of failure, I returned to the woodshed, filled a wheelbarrow with alder chunks and brought it to the shop door.

Feeling an emotional wreck, I tackled my office, organizing loose papers, old letters, and straightening up the bookshelves until my body wore out like my mind. Feeling exhausted, I went to bed.

Early in the morning, at the time I had planned to begin writing about practical happiness, I couldn't. Instead, I found the rake and began dragging leaves off the road that leads to the creek. After a couple of hours, my wife came down to see me. We cried together and talked as I continued raking for another hour. She offered to fix me breakfast. It sounded great.

While eating, my daughters cheerfully asked if I was going to write that day. I didn't ever want to write again, especially on practical happiness! I told them I just couldn't.

After breakfast I cleaned the shop, emptied the back of my truck, organized and sharpened tools. I needed these things done before my next job. I felt like Peter after Jesus died; he just wanted to go back to fishing and minding his own business.

I convinced myself I was unfit for writing. What did I have to say about happiness when I hadn't maintained it in my own home? That's when I heard God's voice in my heart, "I didn't ask you to write because you were perfect. I've shown you a measure of truth and I want you to write it regardless of how you feel. I want you to write what you've seen."

The next day I walked through an organized shop into a clean office. Looking out the window I could see the raked road heading to the creek. Upstairs my wife and daughters slept; we had grown closer together, facing our shortcomings through the bond of love. With my hair brushed and face washed, I began writing the lessons I had seen.

What appeared like an irreparable mess on Monday night had worked its way into a sound lesson by Wednesday morning, not to mention giving me the motivation to clean up my clutter.

Maybe someday I'll grow up and learn how to keep completely away from discouragement. But for now, I'll have to be content knowing one way to get out of it once it comes upon me.

Though thinking is important, what a man does with his hands declares what he is. Therefore, I place more merit on a man's actions than on the clarity of his thought. Isaac might be wild with fear and still rescue his sister from the river. Brendan could be wallowing in a world of self-pity yet help his grandma carry in her groceries. John may feel like never getting out of bed again, but rise to feed the animals that depend upon him.

I try to keep a healthy mind by memorizing, meditating, calculating, and thinking about good things. Nevertheless, when it gets out of control and seems like it's going crazy, I don't worry about it anymore. I tell God every detail of my feelings, ask for help, consider my responsibilities, and warm up by doing the easy ones. This course of action has proven effective whenever I follow it. In addition, I'm encouraged by all the projects that get completed during confusing times in my mind.

May you always have a stable mind; however, if it should ever seem to get shaky, keep your shoes tied.

Even a child is known by his doings, whether his work be pure, and whether it be right.
(Proverbs 20:11)

Questions

- Define *responsibility*.

- How does being responsible help a weak mind?

- What did "Keep your shoes tied" mean?

- What's more important than thinking straight and feeling good?

Chapter 30

A Business Tip

The best preparation for the future is the
present well seen to, and the last duty done.

—George MacDonald

During the 1970s, residential construction in Oregon ran wild. Wherever you looked, tradesmen raced to build houses. It seemed like everybody and their dog considered buying a contractor's license, a tool belt, and a pickup truck.

By 1980, the housing market had dried up. Many builders moved to Alaska or Texas. Those who stayed in town began remodeling and lived on half their former income.

In 1985, builders were back again with enough work to go around. Home building prospered, but many contractors, especially those who had endured the hard times, feared their prosperity wouldn't last. They took jobs they didn't need and couldn't easily complete. It pushed them into working long hours and weekends.

Since 2000, construction has been wild again. Owners and their dogs are obtaining licenses and the get-every-job mentality still prevails. The contractor who used to build four houses a year is trying for ten. The company able to build ten a year is going for twenty. Fear that the market may fade drives contractors to get as much work as they possibly can.

Many companies have concentrated so intently on generating more work that they've forgotten why they're getting it. A common greeting these days is, "Are you keeping busy?" when maybe it should be, "Are you enjoying your work?"

Some contractors remind me of a dog straining against a chain that's attached to a stake in the ground. With a collar burning the hair off their throat, they run at chain's length in repeated circles on a self-made dirt track, barking at who knows what while knocking over their food dish and water bucket with the line. They don't seem to know why they run; they just run.

In contrast I imagine a wiser dog, though chained like the first, lying quietly by the stake, patiently waiting for his owner. At the sight of the man, the dog rises to a sitting position. A slightly wagging tail betrays his pleasure. The man unhooks the collar, turns toward the trail leading to the river, and gently says, "Heel." Delighted to be with his master, the dog watches his every step. Side by side they walk through the grass, around trees and over logs until they reach the river bank. "Sit," says the master. "Stay." The man walks a few yards, pulls a ball from his pocket and throws it into the water. Looking back he sees the dog's eyes riveted on the floating object. Every muscle quivers in anticipation. "Fetch," commands the man. From an exploding cloud of rocks, sand, and grass, the dog races toward the water, leaping, swimming, grasping, paddling back, and dropping the ball at the master's feet. With a pat for the dog's head and with mutual respect, the man says, "Good dog." A tail wags on the grass.

Which of these two dogs would you rather be? When it comes to business, most men live like dog number one, unaware that God designed business to be like dog number two. If dogs could talk, number one would ask through his panting, "Are you

keeping busy?" while number two would quietly inquire, "Do you enjoy your work?"

This past spring I watched it happen again. An eager contractor signed a contract with a couple to build their home. He began with enthusiasm, however in a few months it bored him and he accepted another job. When the completion date for the first house went by and the house was nowhere near finished, the owners became angry. These owners were nice folks but the contractor pushed them too far. Not only did he push the homeowners over the edge, many of the sub-contractors went too.

I won't go into all the particular troubles this man caused his customers, sub-contractors, and himself. It's enough to say that I'm surprised that he didn't end up in jail. His eagerness to obtain a job he wouldn't finish, his desire for money without corresponding work, and his neglect of the responsibilities at hand made a mess in everyone's world.

I chatted with that contractor one day when we met off the job site. He said he was glad to be finished with that project and was thoroughly enjoying his new ones. The only trouble was that the first one wasn't completely finished. He left a lot of hard feelings behind and a line of people that will never work with him again.

"Thou shalt not covet,"[1] though spoken by God thousands of years ago, still applies to contractors today. God knew that following His ways would create quietness, order, rest, and happiness. His wisdom is timeless. Grasping for things—a job, fame, or fortune—rather than concentrating on fulfilling your responsibilities will almost always end in a struggle.[2]

Here's a practical business tip that comes from hearing God's commandment and watching builders like the one I described: If you want a happy company and customers, don't concentrate on getting jobs. Set your attention upon *completing* the work at hand. Put off new starts, avoid new promises. If you can't get to all the projects people want you to do, say no to the newcomers. Don't let new commitments hinder your current work.

Anybody can start a project; even a golden retriever can carry a set of plans to a job site. Few men, however, know how to give a first-rate finish. If your business gets a reputation for completing jobs, you'll never be concerned about getting a job again. Customers will line up and wait for you. And let them wait. Don't allow a new job to distract you from completely, entirely, totally and utterly finishing your present one.

If you want a joyful experience at work, as much as it lies with you, start every project with the eagerness of a new adventure; faithfully give attention to the daily grind; but most of all, I repeat, most of all, with the same eagerness you accepted the job, finish…every…last…detail.

You'll have customers giddy with excitement. They'll shake your hand enough to put tendonitis in your elbow. They'll offer

---

1. Exodux 20:17
2. James 4:1

gifts, pay more than you charged, and glow with happiness. Neighbors will openly lament that they wished their contractor had been so thorough. It sounds like an exaggeration, but it's not! When you finish a job strong and complete, it's a thrill for everybody involved. It's like an extinct animal coming back into existence!

Not everyone or every dog will be a building contractor. These truths about coveting and contentment apply to every sphere of life. Whether in personal affairs or in business, if you want a quiet, peaceable, and happy life, be content with what you have. Don't worry about what's in the future. Finish what you start. You'll never regret making this a personal and business strategy.

> ***Better is the end of a thing than the beginning thereof: and the patient in spirit is better than the proud in spirit.***
> (Ecclesiastes 7:8)

Questions

- What's one reason some building contractors overbook jobs?

- Would you like to be like dog one or dog two? Why?

- Why did the contractor get in trouble?

- What is the business tip?

- How does "Thou shalt not covet" apply to that tip?

Chapter 31

Under His Smile

To be made aware that God is pleased with me,
that His smile rests on me—no language has been
too ardent to express the joy and the strength
which has followed the realization of this.

—Arthur W. Robinson

Is your dad delighted with you? Is he pleased by what you're doing? Do his eyes light up when you enter the room? When something comes between you and your dad, do you know how to make it right? Do you live in the sunshine of his smile?

Living in the light of a father's smile is one of the grandest experiences in the world. Sadly, few people get that privilege. Many families are damaged, and one generation is often at odds with the next. Nevertheless, within every one of us is a desire to dwell with a happy father. The longing isn't limited to boys. A man longs for a joyful relationship with his father from the day he's born until the day he dies. Anger and bitterness over past injuries may completely bury the feeling, but they never remove it. God made us with a hunger to live with a happy father.

Many people see God, especially what they call the God of the Old Testament, as hard to please and easily angered. They imagine Him as distant, requiring impossible standards, and poised to punish any who fail.

Those ideas are far from the truth. The God of the Old Testament is the same One who showed Himself, in the New Testament, through Jesus. He is the happiest Being ever. His smile drives away darkness. To those who welcome Him, He's the warmth of sunshine and the freshness of a spring breeze. His songs and laughter flood the universe.

As the Father of creation, He knows not just the importance, but the wonder, grandeur, and magnificence of happy relationships between fathers and children.[1] That's why He wrote the book of Leviticus.

Leviticus? Isn't that a stuffy outdated book about Jewish sacrificial laws?

To the blind it is. But to a man with understanding, it's a guide to experiencing the greatest adventure available to man, which is living under the continual smile of God's radiant face. Leviticus, along with every other book in the Bible, gives men the tools, instruction, and assurance whereby they might look into their Creator's eyes, sigh with pleasure, and bask in His kindness.

God gave Israel sacrificial ceremonies. These ceremonies describe His desire for delightful relationships with people, our steps to attain it, and what to do when we fall short. Living under God's smile is clear, simple, affordable, and available for anyone willing to accept it.

Leviticus chapter 4 outlined for Israel how to respond after they had ignorantly sinned, at the first awareness of their fault. Whether it was a priest, a ruler, a common man, or the whole congregation who had missed the mark, God gave specific steps to provide for thorough restoration.

When a common man felt a twinge of guilt, warning that his actions had separated him from God's favor, the law required him to bring a female goat kid, without blemish, to the priest,

---

1. Malachi 3:5-6

lay his hand upon its head and kill it at the place of burnt offerings. The priest was supposed to take the blood with his finger,
put it on the horns of the altar, pour out the rest of the blood
at the bottom of the altar, and take away all the fat and burn it.
By following these simple acts, the Israelites enjoyed complete
assurance of forgiveness.

It wasn't like today's tax laws that require a lawyer's judgment and an accountant's degree to arrive at an, "I think this will
work" solution, "but keep your records for seven years, just in
case it doesn't." The Israelites had absolutely *no* questions. They

knew what to do. A paved, well-lit road lined with readable signs directed every repentant man to forgiveness; everyone knew it.

Who knows why God chose certain heifers, hyssop, blood, unleavened bread, oil, burning of the fat, and all the other specific methods and requirements. There's no reason to question the methods. He's the Boss and has every right to make the rules. These were the rules He chose.

Even though He used these methods, the New Testament says that God had no pleasure in burnt offerings and sacrifices for sin.[1] If not, what was the meaning of all those laws and sacrifices? They were just tools, tools to teach His people a lesson they'd never forget. This was the lesson: There is a way to come to God whereby you can know for sure whether you stand forgiven and accepted in His sight, or whether you don't. It was a way to remove *all* doubts and questions. These ceremonies offered complete assurance of right-standing with God to all who would follow them, and complete assurance of separation from God to all those who wouldn't.

The vast amount of repeated details bores me a little in some places because I don't understand them. It might happen as you read also. Though each item is important, don't get hung up in the particulars and miss the message of a loving God providing a doubt-proof method of reconciliation.

These sacrifices were a shadow of Jesus, who is the reality. The book of Hebrews taught the Jews that their intense assurance found in the sacrificial cleansing is all the more assured by their trust in Jesus. "If the blood of bulls and of goats and the ashes of an heifer sprinkling the unclean, sanctifieth to the purifying of the flesh: How much more shalt the blood of Christ, who through the eternal Spirit offered himself without spot to God, purge your conscience from dead works to serve the living God?"[2]

We now trust, not in animal sacrifices, but upon God's once and for all sacrifice in Jesus. We are told that "If we confess our sins, He is faithful and just to forgive us our sins and to cleanse

---

1. Hebrews 9
2. Hebrews 9:13-14

us from all unrighteousness."[1] Following the specific laws of sacrifices gave complete assurance to the Israelites. Now, by agreeing with God that we have fallen short and that He already paid the price in Jesus, our consciences are even more assured of His favor. He's the One with the right to make the rules; our job is to accept and obey.

Realizing these things is the sprinkling that cleanses us from a destructive conscience.[2] An evil conscience will say, "You're not good enough. God doesn't want you. Clean up your life before trying to come to Him. There's no hope for you." When we believe God's rules, we don't have to listen to those lies any more.

The basis for true happiness is that God is happy and kind. It's possible to always walk in His cheerful light. Should things ever begin to get dark, we have a simple, sure remedy: confess our sins and enjoy the cleansing. As we experience these truths, the common longing to have a warm relationship with a father melts into rest, just as the frantic chick finds relief at last by diving into the feathers of the hen. His love and our hunger are a perfect match.

You don't want to leave words and truths about God on pages in dusty books. They're meant to live. Being made in His image, you have the privilege to offer folks the same acceptance His smile brings to you.

Many of you will be dads someday. Shine the light of your face upon your children. Bring warmth and laughter into your home. When anyone begins to feel guilty or distant from you, give them clear steps to restore oneness. Assure them that you're available day or night. Regardless of their attitude, pursue a delightful relationship with each one. Until you have children of your own, practice on your siblings, parents, and neighbors.

When the theology of God becomes a part of your everyday life, you'll radiate with joy and be an encouragement to many.

I wish someone had told me when I was a kid that the intense longing I had to please my dad was a gift to draw me to

---

1. 1 John 1:9
2. Hebrews 10:22

my Father in heaven. Like most children, at times I desired more from my dad than he could give. Now with the complete assurance of my heavenly Father's pleasure, I'm free to appreciate my earthly father more.

> *Purge me with hyssop, and I shall be clean:*
> *Wash me, and I shall be whiter than snow.*
> *Make me to hear joy and gladness;*
> *That the bones which thou hast broken may*
>   *rejoice.*
> *Hide thy face from my sins,*
> *And blot out all mine iniquities.*
> *Create in me a clean heart; O God*
> *And renew a right spirit in me.*
> *Cast me not away from thy presence;*
> *And take not thy holy spirit from me.*
> *Restore unto me the joy of thy salvation;*
> *And uphold me with thy free spirit.*
> *Then will I teach transgressors thy ways;*
> *And sinners shall be converted unto thee.*

(Psalm 51:7-13)

Questions

- Who gave us the longing to be loved by our dad?

- How did He plan to fulfill that longing?

- What did God do to assure the Jews He was approachable?

- How do we come to God now?

- In what practical ways can we express this theology?

Chapter 32

Remember

Practical wisdom, for the purpose of life, must be carried about with us, and be ready for use at call. It is not sufficient that we have a fund laid up at home, but not a farthing in the pocket: we must carry about with us a store of the current coin of knowledge ready for exchange on all occasions else we are comparatively helpless when the opportunity for action occurs.

—Samuel Smiles

You need an MRI," the doctor said. "I'll schedule it. You're not claustrophobic are you?"

"I don't think so," I replied.

Claustrophobia is the fear of being in tight places. I get uncomfortable squeezing my way between furnace ducts and plumbing pipes to the far reaches of a spider-infested crawl space of a house, but I don't think you call that claustrophobia.

MRI stands for Magnetic Resolution Imagery. It's an amazing technological advancement that somehow uses whirling magnets to project images of your body onto a computer screen. The patient is stuffed into a tube, and virtually sliced into thin strips. A doctor can flip through the pictures like thumbing through a stack of sliced baloney and pull out the one that will best show the patient's problem. With that information, he can offer his best course of treatment.

I called the imaging company to confirm the scheduled date. "You're not claustrophobic are you?" the scheduler asked.

"No, I don't think so," I answered. Was I supposed to be?

The next day as I filled out papers in the waiting room, the receptionist asked, "You're not claustrophobic are you?"

"I hope not," I replied.

A few minutes later I sat on the edge of the conveyor belt listening to last-minute instructions. The technician asked, "Are you claustrophobic?"

"I don't know, I used to not think so, but you guys are wearing me down. Maybe I am!"

"If you have any problems just call and we'll drag you out."

As the belt moved me into the machine, my arms pushed lightly against my sides. My heart rate increased and my breathing shortened. Through earphones the tech told me to lie still; in forty-five minutes we'd be done.

I could sense God speaking, "As the walls of this machine are getting tight around you, life is going to become tight also. Relax. I'm going to use the MRI machine of life to take a picture of your heart."

Before the test was over, I had almost fallen asleep.

In the weeks that followed, life did tighten up. Pain in my back and legs increased until I could no longer walk without sweating and nearly fainting. Often, I couldn't fall asleep at night until exhaustion overcame me at five or six in the morning.

The living room couch and a painful path to the bathroom became the limits of my tight place.

One morning after midnight I read Psalm 77. David said, "In the day of my trouble I sought the Lord." I paused to look up *trouble* in a Hebrew dictionary. It came from the root word meaning "to be in a tight place."

Curious to know what David did when he found himself in a tight spot, I continued reading and discovered a practical secret. Here is what he wrote: "I remembered God...I have considered the days of old...I call to remembrance my song in the night...I will remember the works of the Lord...I will remember the wonders of old…I will meditate also of all thy work, and talk of thy doings."[1] In the second half of the psalm, he recorded some of the things he remembered.

For the next few hours I experimented with David's secret. I began recalling all the times I had run out of things and how God provided. I remembered running out of gas near the only open gas station within 250 miles, running out of food one day and finding my cupboards mysteriously stuffed in the evening, running out of carpentry tools through the hands of thieves and getting a tremendous job falling timber. I reviewed the times I ran out of money, time, favor, and peace and remembered how God meet every need.

I reviewed broken bones, smashed fingers, strained muscles, strange internal pains, and even a previous time when I couldn't walk and how I had healed from each event.

Long before recalling all the wonderful things I had seen God do, I had complete assurance that He would care for me in my current tight spot. I fell asleep in peace.

On the landing in our stairway hangs a thin cabinet protected from dust by a glass door. The little shelves are filled with tokens of remembrance. A set of old points from the distributor of my '77 Ford pickup reminds me of the time we broke down in our driveway thirty minutes from town. Not being a mechanic and never before working on an ignition system, my wife and I were shocked when I guessed the problem, found a new set of points in the barn, and installed them. The truck ran like a dream.

On one shelf is a picture of a dismantled washing machine. I tried to give that appliance away and nobody would take it. I even offered to pay a guy to haul it off and he wouldn't. It contained concrete ballast blocks and was too heavy to move by myself. I tore it to pieces and found my wife's engagement and wedding rings at the bottom. She had lost them two years before. Who could have imagined the value of that unwanted machine!

There is also a picture of the travel trailer we lived in for six years, six teeth a kind dentist removed from Emily's mouth,

---

1. Psalm 77:2 ff.

and a copy of the key my wife locked inside my in-law's car in the parking lot of the local Bi-Mart. Now that I think about it, almost every item in that memory box relates to a time of trouble and what God did to relieve it.

One of the privileges of getting older is having not only a box but a mind full of great times that first appeared in the disguise of trouble. It happens so often that I'm starting to anticipate the good times while still in the middle of difficulty. My confidence today is based upon the memories of watching God turn past problems into opportunities.

That's why on my way home from work last Monday I could rejoice. While driving at 35 mph and minding my own business, it sounded like five linebackers jumped in the back of my truck and began pounding on the bed with sledge hammers! A quick look in my side mirror revealed a four-inch-wide stripe of rear-end grease trailing me down the road. I almost made it to the shoulder before coming to a stop. "This is going to be a good memory," I thought; and it is.

A young man with a cell phone stood across the street from where I parked. He allowed me to call AAA towing. Many kind folks stopped to offer assistance and tell me that they had used rear ends for sale if I needed one. The police placed flares around me as darkness approached. I sat in the driver's seat for a couple of hours making a list of all the good things that happened. What I looked forward to the most was seeing Al, my mechanic. It had been months since my car or truck needed repair.

Later that night, the tow truck unloaded my rig at Al's. And just like I had hoped Al and I had a great time together catching up on what God was doing in each of our lives.

What looked like trouble turned into a story for my journal, a knick-knack for the shelf, and a one more memory block for the foundation of my faith. Next time you find yourself in a tight spot, remember what God has done in the past for you and others—it's the pathway to rest.

Should you ask me in the future, "Are you claustrophobic?" the answer is no.

My soul shall be satisfied as with marrow and fatness; and my mouth shall praise thee with joyful lips: When I remember thee upon my bed, and meditate on thee in the night watches.

(Psalm 63:5-6)

Questions

- What's an MRI?

- What does *claustrophobic* mean?

- How did David overcome the fears and discouragement of trouble?

- What can you do to help remember the good things God has done?

- What is one story you remember about God helping you in a time of trouble?

Chapter 33

Conscience

Nothing between my soul and the Savior,
So that His blessed face may be seen;
Nothing preventing the least of His favor,
Keep the way clear! Let nothing between.

—Charles A. Tindley

"You really want me to take it?" asked Brian in surprise.

He had been helping a neighbor clean out the shed in her backyard. Against one wall stood an old Honda 55 motorcycle covered with dust and spiderwebs. As Brian grabbed the handlebars and pushed it forward so he could sweep under it, Mrs. Miller suggested, "Why don't you take that machine home? My son lives in Delaware now and hasn't touched it for over twenty years. Do you want it?"

Did he want it? Of course he wanted it! Wow, this would be great! "Are you sure you want me to have it?" asked Brian again.

"Please take it; I'll have more room when it's gone."

After completing his job, Brian wheeled the bike home. He could already imagine his hand on the throttle and the wind in his face. He wanted to get it running as soon as possible.

"Let's see," he thought to himself, "I need to check the oil and probably change it. The gas tank needs rinsing and some new fuel put in. Maybe I'll take a look at the spark plug."

As Brian pushed the bike into the driveway, a light rain began to fall. The garage was full, and the porch was too small. He had an idea, "Nobody's home. Maybe I could take this thing into the kitchen and work on it there. I'd be warm and out of the rain." A quick picture of his mom's face crossed his mind, but in his excitement he paid no attention.

Through the back door, past the washer and dryer and into the kitchen he maneuvered his new bike. He noticed the brown stripe on the floor that followed him in. Immediately he thought of his little sister Mary, who was on floor duty that week. "Oh, she wouldn't mind," he reasoned.

He thought the same thing when the picture of his older sister Julie came to mind as he grabbed her towel to wipe dirt off the gas tank and when a fleeting snapshot of his dad appeared as he got out his father's personal toolbox.

Thoroughly engrossed in his project, Brian didn't notice his family returning until all four of them entered the kitchen. As Mary looked at the floor, Julie at her towel, Dad at the tools, and Mom viewed the whole mess, the four demanded as one, "*What are you doing?*"

Brian's answer didn't help matters any, "Well, you never made a rule that I couldn't work on motorcycles in the kitchen!" As you can imagine, things got worse before they got better. Brian had missed something in his thought process that created a cloud between himself and every other person in his family.

Do you remember reading about Leviticus 4 in a previous chapter? Its main idea is responding to your first twinge of guilt; at the moment you realize something is between you and God, take steps to remove the growing wall.

During the Sermon on the Mount, Jesus taught that when you first realize your brother has something against you, stop what you're doing, even if it's worshipping God, and quickly make it right.

These two ideas align with God's basic rules for genuine Christianity: Love God with all your heart and love your neighbor as yourself. At the first awareness that either of these two relationships are fading, make steps of restoration.

God has given each of us a tremendous tool that detects when something comes between us and God, or between us and other people. It's called a conscience. A warning sounds within us. Sometimes it's as loud as a car's burglar alarm in a parking garage, other times as faint as a termite chewing in the wall. It's especially quiet when we are headlong into obtaining strong desires.

As Brian pushed his cycle into the kitchen, a picture of his mother ran through his mind. That was his conscience saying, "You are bringing a motorcycle between you and your mom." The same warning came when Brian used the floor, towel, and tools without regard to the feelings of his family members.

There is no rule in the Bible that says you can't make muddy stripes on the utility room floor; however, you can be sure it's wrong when the act damages a relationship. As a general rule, whatever clouds a friendship with God and others is wrong. Whatever brightens the relationship of everyone involved is right. God gave us a conscience to help maintain good relationships.

The apostle Paul said, "Herein do I exercise myself, to have always a conscience void of offense toward God, and toward man."[1] Paul didn't carry around a list of dos and don'ts. He didn't flip through his notebook searching for the right course of action for each situation he faced. Instead, he possessed a simple instrument—a conscience—to determine the best course for action.

When dealing with the Corinthians and their struggles with meat offered to idols, Paul's conclusions were based on the uncomplicated formula: Will it cloud my brother's relationship with me or with God?[2] Avoid it if it does. Allow it if it doesn't.

There's no law in the Bible about pounding on drums inside of houses. Suppose you feel like tapping out a little marching music. After strapping on your snare drum and picking up the sticks, you enter the living room. That's when you notice your mom soothing her headache by resting on the couch. To play or not to play? That is the question. If you have the slightest smidgeon of a conscience, it will tell you that something is about to come between you and your mom if you let one stick so much as touch any part of that drum. It's not right or wrong based on

1. Acts 24:16
2. 1 Corinthians 8

a rule; it's good or bad based on what it will do for your relationship. After your conscience's warning, you might choose to pull down the shade and tiptoe from the room.

You'll often encounter situations where there are no written rules for conduct. Taking heed to your conscience will help prevent you from foolish actions. When you sense the warning, stop and consider: Will my actions darken my relations with God and people, or will it brighten them? Choose the brightest path and go for it!

At the time of Christ, in the center of the temple was a room called the Holy of Holies. There between two cherubim statues stood the Ark of the Covenant. If there ever was a place that could be called God's residence, this was it. A veil separated this room from the rest of the temple. Only once a year did a priest enter, to offer atoning blood.

The moment Jesus died, that veil mysteriously ripped from top to bottom. This physical miracle showed that the spiritual wall between God and man no longer existed. Jesus had reconciled the two. That's the work of love. Today Jesus' life continues drawing people to God and uniting them with one another.

God invites us to join Him in this reconciling work.[1] Armed with a conscience that warns us before we damage relationships and His voice that gives us creative ways to remove walls that separate people, we are well-equipped for a delightful adventure.

A word of caution, it's possible to sear your conscience. If you stick your finger onto a hot stove burner and leave it there for a few moments, you'll sear the skin. Scarred flesh doesn't have the sensitivity soft skin does. In the same way you can sear your conscience by disregarding its warnings. An "I don't care" attitude toward God and those around you will eventually eliminate your ability to sense when your actions are wrong. Unable to detect the timely warnings, you'll damage relationships and possibly shipwreck your life.[2]

Some folks develop oversensitive consciences. They can't walk across the lawn for fear that they might step on a worm or

---

1. 2 Corinthians 5:17-20
2. 1 Timothy 1:19

a bug. As with everything, balance is important. Both seared and oversensitive consciences are troublesome. One tip that might be helpful to maintaining a healthy conscience is to remember that this tool's main use is to warn us before we wrong somebody or to convict us after we have.

Back to Brian and his motorcycle. Though he's an imaginary character, you don't have to go far to find someone like him. When he refused to listen to his conscience, his family ganged up against him. He knew better, but disregarded the warnings because he was too intent upon his own desires. If he continues rejecting his conscience, before long he won't have the benefit of that faithful friend. Nor any real friends at all for that matter!

May you have a healthy conscience and a desire to heed its warning. You'll find it a sure guide to joyful relationships with people and most importantly with God.

> *Happy is he that condemneth not himself in that thing which he alloweth.*
> (Romans 14:22)

Questions

- How did Brian's conscience try to warn him about the bike in the kitchen?

- Why didn't he listen?

- What does the conscience mainly warn us about?

- What are the two great commandments?

- How does our conscience help us to align with those commandments?

- What action sears a conscience?

Chapter 34

A Lie

What dominates [a man's] consciousness on the street or in the store, will dominate it when he is on his knees. He will try to direct his mind toward God. But his mind will be full of thoughts of things, and desires for things, and fears of loss of things, and schemes to acquire things. He will if he thinks of God at all, try to make God his agent in the acquisition of things. So he will never have real fellowship with God.

—Albert Edward Day, *Discipline and Discovery*

Since the beginning of time, one particular lie has robbed men of happiness. Its deception is as powerful today as ever. What's sad about this particular lie is not that it prevents a man from being joyful, but that it steals the joy he already has.

Here is the lie: **You do not possess enough to be happy.** It started in the Garden of Eden and has spread to every corner of the world.

The snake told Eve that she was missing out on life. He said that if she ate the fruit, it would open her eyes and she'd be like a god, knowing good and evil.[1]

---

1. Genesis 3

Thinking she couldn't possibly be happy without having everything, Eve bit into the morsel and gave some to Adam. Their eyes were opened; however, they didn't receive the happiness they sought. Instead, they found sorrow and death, not only for themselves, but for all their descendants.

The apostle Paul had a young friend named Timothy. As an older man desiring the younger's success, Paul shared some of the wisdom he had gained through the words of Jesus and through personal experiences. Can you see the similarities between Adam and Eve's experience and this warning Paul gave to Timothy: "But they that will be rich fall into temptation and a snare, and into many foolish and hurtful lusts, which drown men in destruction and perdition. For the love of money is the root of all evil: which while some coveted after, they have erred from the faith, and pierced themselves through with many sorrows."[1]

Paul didn't make up these words as a catchy piece of advice. Surely, he had watched it happen. It might have been part of the reason he insisted on working with his own hands, to provide not only his needs, but those of his fellow workers as well.[2]

What tempted Adam and Eve, and faced Paul and Timothy, tempts you and me today. We all have a strong, God-given desire to be happy. The trouble is, allured by false imposters, we often miss the happiness we seek.

One prominent lie is that you cannot be happy unless you own your own house. Any more, you don't have to *own* the house to gain this alleged happiness; you merely have to talk someone into loaning you the money for a mortgage. Many young men think having a house is essential to win or keep a wife. Though it may appear so, true happiness is not found in houses.

For a number of years I worked in one of Eugene's premier neighborhoods. It's a street where folks would drive on weekends just to look at the fancy houses and dream of how great it would be to live in one.

Mr. R., a prominent businessman in town, built on the corner. As his house neared completion, he filed bankruptcy. The laws freed him from all his debts and prevented creditors from

---

1. 1 Timothy 6:9-10
2. Acts 20:33-35

taking his residence. A law designed to protect a man from homelessness became a rich man's method of getting a huge house without paying for it.

Across the street lived Mr. P. in a palatial monument. Though beautiful on the outside, the edifice reminded me of a courthouse, not from its beauty but from the volume of lawsuits that plagued the subcontractors and owner alike.

Next door was what we called the Adam's Family house, a spooky looking place. The last time I drove by, though a new house, it stood empty, surrounded by a chain-link fence and the mystery of what went wrong. One known trouble was the wealthy builder. He faced citywide embarrassment when caught submitting bills to the client for materials used on his own house.

Across the street, weeds grew around an abandoned foundation, huge enough for a grocery store. The owners, mad at the city, quit building in the middle of their project and moved thirty miles north.

There are many other stories of people and houses on that street; these are enough to give you a feeling of the atmosphere behind the front doors.

After decades of building residences, I've concluded that owning houses does not make people happy, especially fancy houses. I've seen happier people renting mobile homes than most folks in expensive houses. There are exceptions. Those are the people who may live in a beautiful house but save their affections for more important things. Their riches increased, but they didn't set their heart upon them.

Daniel Gilbert, a Harvard researcher, has attempted to understand what he calls "affective forecasting." Through laboratory and field tests, he scientifically examined the way people look into the future and predict and act upon what they think will make them happy or unhappy—and how they felt afterwards about those predictions and actions.

His conclusion,

Happiness…is elusive. We may predict that a bigger salary or a fancier car will make us happy, but the outcome is that the happiness, the excitement about having that salary or car, wears off. What happens is that we adapt. Yet in making our affective forecasts, we tend to forget that we will adapt. Time and again, we're led by false expectations of pleasure to make choices that ultimately make us no happier, a process [called]…"miswanting."

Every decision we make is [based] on our belief that one course of action is going to make us happier than another…So it's pretty common for people to be in love with a particular consumer good—say, a new car. They get the new car, and what happens? Well, for a little while, there's a lot of joy. Then that joy fades very quickly. What a person might conclude is… "Things don't really bring me the happiness I thought." But that is not what Americans conclude by and large because, as members of a consumer society, the conclusion is, "It must not have been the right car. I probably need an even better one."

You have to understand that people are trying to be as happy as possible. But societies, particularly consumer societies like ours, are not designed to make people as happy as possible. They are designed to make them consume as much as possible.

Since people want happiness and societies want consumption, it is the job of society to convince people that consumption equals happiness. Otherwise, they are going to stop [consuming]. So the message we are getting from every billboard, every magazine, every television show, every commercial is that more stuff equals more happiness. Pretty hard to resist that message when it is coming at you several hours per day.[1]

I'm glad Mr. Gilbert did his research. His description of the problem is super. Thousands of years ago, the Bible (It's such a great Book!) described the same trouble. Two consumers were tricked by a false advertiser. The same lie Adam and Eve fell for and Paul

1. Wanda Urbanska and Frank Levering, *Nothing's Too Small to Make a Difference* (Winston-Salem, NC: John F. Blair, 2004), p. 19. (This book is not from a biblical Christian point of view though it does hold many true principles.)

warned Timothy about, Mr. Gilbert concluded we all tend to fall for. The actual lures have changed, but the lie remains the same.

I like the challenge of laboratory research and field experiments. Discovering how God designed us fascinates me. If a researcher fails to include the Creator in his calculations, the summary may contain many facts, yet slightly miss the mark. These errors often negate the useful application of research.

The quoted study stated happiness was elusive. That's very true when applied to consumer products. If we increase the scope of investigation to include a Creator, happiness is no longer elusive. There is an unchanging fountain for joy, cheerfulness, and delight. They flow like cold, clear, and refreshing water from one source alone—the heart of God.

Jesus contrasted consumer happiness with God's happiness when He told the woman at the well, "Whosoever drinketh of this water shall thirst again: But whosoever drinketh of the water that I shall give him shall never thirst; but the water I shall give him shall be in him a well of water springing up into everlasting life."[1]

As an older man, I'm writing to you younger men, attempting to convince you that a man's life does not consist in the abundance of the things he possesses.[2] God knows you need food. He knows you need clothes. Jesus promised you would have both.[3] Riches will come and go. If you set your heart on them, you'll be elated and depressed as they rise and fall.

You have been—and will be—lied to. When you hear the words, "Get this and you'll be happy!" don't fall for it! Paul told Timothy, "But godliness with contentment is great gain. For we brought nothing into this world, and it is certain we can carry nothing out, and having food and raiment let us be therewith content."[4]

If you learn to set your affections upon God, you'll avoid the heartbreaks that result from chasing elusive dreams of pleasure. Moreover, you'll discover the fountain[5] from Whom all happiness flows.

---

1. John 4:13-14
2. Luke 12:15
3. Matthew 6:25-34
4. 1 Timothy 6:6-8
5. Exodus 17:1-7; Numbers 20:1-11; 1 Corinthians 10:4

O Timothy, keep that which is committed to thy trust, avoiding profane and vain babblings, and oppositions of science falsely so called: which some professing have erred concerning the faith. Grace be with thee. Amen.

(1 Timothy 6:20-21)

Questions

- What is one lie that plagued Adam and Eve and still troubles people today?

- What does "affective forecasting" mean? What do people usually forget to include in their "forecasts"?

- The Bible tells us to be content if we have two things. What are they?

- If you have these two things and godliness also, what do you have?

- The scientific study concluded that happiness was elusive. Is that true? Why?

Chapter 35

The Seriousness of Murmuring

God is not bound to subject his ways of operation to the scrutiny of our thoughts.

—John Locke

When he ended the conversation, I hung up the phone with sadness in my spirit. The call wasn't unusual. I've listened to many before. The men on the other end have been single or married, old or young, some prosperous in business while others appear like failures. Their life situations don't seem to make a difference. The common thread is that they all describe a frustrated life.

Last night, the young man on the other end began by saying that he wanted advice on how to return to the old paths. For thirty minutes he covered a number of topics. He lamented there were few men he respected. Most Christian leaders he knows have been poor fathers. The failures of their children negate his ability to receive their advice. Maybe one or two could be trusted to give acceptable counsel.

He bemoaned that men who should be in authority are neglecting it. He reasoned that maybe a few guys like himself should place themselves under negligent leaders in an attempt to get them to start leading, the way a wife might try to lead her husband into leading.

He continued to bewail parents who won't let their children get married. He reasoned that over-cautious parents put a tremendous strain on young men when they refuse them their daughters. Thwarted, the unmarried young men have to fight alone against moral temptations. If parents, he reasoned, would only loosen up and give away their daughters, the young men wouldn't have the problems they do.

As the long distance minutes ticked by, his murmuring went to the church. It isn't producing godly members, especially in the young men. Next, it was how our society weakens Christians, offers poor role models, and captures the younger generation.

He concluded by saying that when he looks at declining America, he's left with a measure of hopelessness and despair. He wondered how he could succeed surrounded with such darkness.

After thirty minutes, he said that he had to go back to work and asked if he could call again the next time he needed some advice.

The young man told me he had a learner's attitude, yet never once asked what I thought about any of his topics. They were the same topics he struggled with a year ago, and will be the same ones he faces ten years from now unless something drastically changes him.

The laments I usually hear are about the poor government we have, the lack of opportunities to fulfill dreams, troublesome jobs or no jobs at all, troublesome wives or no wife at all. They blame their town, their parents, their education, their churches, their friends, and though they rarely come right out and say it, God Himself. It's always somebody else's fault why life isn't the way they want it.

After reading these lamenting paragraphs, doesn't it put a weight on your shoulders? I cannot imagine the drain of daily viewing life from a complaining perspective.

If I ever got the chance to offer my thoughts on the matter I'd have to say, "Maybe you should consider becoming a Christian." I can imagine the indignant sputtering, "What do you mean? I've been a Christian for years!" Without the theological debates over what happens when you ask Jesus into your heart or when is the point of salvation, the man who lives as a murmurer is not submitted to the lordship of Jesus. Without a restful submission, without unreserved trust that the Lord is the Lord of all, there's no hope of living in light or joy.

A murmurer's god is small. He's not big enough to work through local governments, let alone move kings. He can't set boundaries for every storm or provide provisions when needed. His god can't bring a wife at the proper time, work within a parent's decision, or show his glory in spite of a corrupt church. A murmurer's god is often thwarted by Satan's will and thereby fails to provide a place of rest for his followers.

If your god is a weakling like I just described, you had better find the One you can trust. Find the One who rules over all. Give up *your* opinions, *your* methods, *your* power, *your* dreams, and *your* superiority; and subject yourself to *Him*!

Get a God like Daniel had. His God happens to be the same One Abraham, Isaac, and Jacob knew. He's the One that breathed life into Adam and instructed Noah to build an ark. Daniel's God sent a foreign king to overthrow his homeland and carry him away captive.[1] His God didn't just allow the king to invade, He sent the king. Under this big God's watchful eye, Daniel became a eunuch, which meant he would never have a family.

God brought Daniel into favor with authorities.[2] He gave him knowledge and skill in all learning and wisdom…understanding in all visions and dreams.[3] After watching Daniel live in submission to God, the conquering king fell upon his face and worshipped Daniel saying, "Of a truth it is, that your God is a God of gods and a Lord of kings."[4] Through this heathen king,

---

1. Jeremiah 29:4
2. Daniel 1:9
3. Daniel 1:17
4. Daniel 2:47

God crowned Daniel as ruler over the chief of the governors, over all the wise men, and over the whole province of Babylon.[1]

When Babylon invaded Israel, Daniel had no idea he would become Babylon's ruler in a few short years. The king chose him above presidents and princes because he had an excellent spirit.

If Daniel had been a murmurer, his thoughts would have run something like this: "Our government is going to the dogs, our rulers are creeps, the church is a mess, and I'll never get the chance to marry. I don't like my job and it looks like national war on the horizon. Woe is me." That Daniel would have never found favor with a foreign king. He would have given up an amazing life for a miserable one. Aren't you glad Daniel wasn't a complainer?

The young man who truly submits himself to God won't complain when God sets the stage around him. Jobs, weather, his parents, the government, current events, and the state of the church, cannot rob his joy, because it's rooted in something bigger than his environment. He doesn't fill his mind with the media, public opinion, and other props. His eye is fixed upon the Director of the world. The young man waits for his part in the play, when the Director says "roll 'em," he's ready with a good attitude, confidence, and a smile. He plays his appointed role and brings honor to the Director.

A murmurer never gets this privilege. He's usually backstage grumbling about his lousy agent, how the scene doesn't suit him, how the other actors don't know their parts, or about the fool he has for makeup and on and on, until the whole show is over and he's left without a part.

If a man's god isn't big enough and good enough to trust for every detail of his life, the man must take up the slack himself. He worries, schemes, and murmurs just like the nation of Israel did while God led them to the Promised Land. They didn't trust Him. With eyes on the wilderness around them, they refused to believe He led them on the best path toward the best goal. They

---

1. Daniel 2:48-49

murmured and complained until God left their bones in the desert. They never set foot in the land of milk and honey.

There is only one God and He controls the events of your life. Whenever you murmur, you murmur against Him. If you've fallen into that foolish practice, you had better quit it today. Look around at your situations, the ones that seem rotten to you; instead of complaining, thank Him for them. You've got all you need to accomplish His best. Submit yourself to His Directorship. Trade your plans for His plans. He doesn't have to explain everything to you. As a follower, it's your job to trust Him no matter where He leads.

If you are unable to cheerfully surrender your lordship for His, you are in serious trouble, not only in this life, but in the life to come. Your only hope is to fall down and cry out, "God, be merciful unto me a sinner."[1]

It may be feeble at first, but if you are serious with God, your conscience will begin to warn you each time you murmur. Take those warnings to heart. Cry to God for the will and power to leave your wicked ways. You cannot afford to spend another minute complaining about your lot in life.

There's a world of confidence, joy, and miracles waiting for the man who will hang up the phone on his complaining and submit himself to the God who rules over all.

Do all things without murmurings and disputings:
that ye may be blameless and harmless, the sons
of God, without rebuke, in the midst of a crooked
and perverse nation, among whom ye shine as
lights in the world; holding forth the word of life.
(Philippians 2:14-16)

---

1. Luke 18:13

Questions

- What size of God does a complainer have?

- Proverbs 17:27 says, "A man of understanding is of an excellent spirit." Daniel had an excellent spirit. What did he understand?

- Who rules the governments that exist in the world today?

- What does God think about complaining and murmuring?

- What should you think about it? Why?

Chapter 36

That Your Joy May Be Full

*Few delights can equal the presence of
one whom we trust utterly.*

—George MacDonald

On the night before Jesus died, the apostle John heard Him make statements like these, "I have spoken unto you, that my joy might remain in you, and that your joy might be full.[1] Hitherto have ye asked nothing in my name: ask and ye shall receive, that your joy may be full...[2] These things I speak in the world, that they might have my joy fulfilled in themselves."[3]

After sixty years of experiencing this life of joy, John wrote a letter that's been preserved in the Bible for almost two thousand years. Here's the introduction to that letter. Can you sense

---

1. John 15:11
2. John 16:24
3. John 17:13

his yearning for others to experience this Life he had come to know?

"That which was from the beginning, which we have heard, which we have seen with our eyes, which we have looked upon, and our hands have handled, of the Word of life; (For the life was manifested, and we have seen it, and bear witness, and show unto you that eternal life, which was with the Father, and was manifested unto us;) That which we have seen and heard declare we unto you, that ye also may have fellowship with us: and truly our fellowship is with the Father, and with his Son Jesus Christ. And these things write we unto you, that your joy may be full."[1]

I've given you many tips about finding happiness in this book you are about to finish. Each chapter relates a seemingly different aspect of joy or cheerfulness. Every one of them attempts to draw you into a clearer understanding of God. There is no other way to fulfill the longing you have for joy than to enter into an abiding relationship with Jesus Christ.

You can spend the rest of your life looking for happiness in every corner of the world and you will fail. No religion can help you. To say that all religions lead to God is a lie. For no religions do. Only a living, abiding relationship with the One who made you can fulfill the longings of your heart and make you whole. It's the way God made it. When you're the Maker you can choose how you want things done. He put a hunger for pleasure within you that can only be filled with His abiding presence. Jesus said that just as a branch cannot bear fruit unless it stays connected to the vine, neither can we experience His joy unless we abide in Him.[2]

Many Christians don't believe God is happy. While some are finding a joy they can hardly contain, others insist that the Christian life is dull. Andrew Murray attempted to describe this in his book, *Abiding in Christ:*

> Christ's own joy, abiding joy, fullness of joy—such
> is the portion of the believer who abides in Christ. Why,

---

1. 1 John 1:1-4
2. John 15:4; Galatians 5:22

O why is it that this joy has so little power to attract? The reason simply is: Men, yea, even God's children, do not believe in it. Instead of the abiding in Christ being looked upon as the happiest life that ever can be led, it is regarded as a life of self-denial and of sadness. They forget that the self-denial and the sadness are [a result of] not abiding, and that to those who once yield themselves unreservedly to abide in Christ as a bright and blessed life, their faith comes true—the joy of the Lord is theirs.[1]

When I think about the joy of the Lord, I have to ask myself, "What makes Him happy right now?" I can't name them all, but here are a few things that are part of His joy. He enjoys the thrill of a bridegroom as He waits for His coming marriage. He knows the joy of a father who once thought his son was dead, but who has now returned. He possesses a rancher's delight in finding a lost sheep.

Imagine knowing that you had recently foiled a terrorist's attempt to destroy everyone in the world. The effort cost your life. You gave the highest expression of love, which is one man laying down his life for another. The chance to die brought joy beyond words.

Consider the happiness that comes to a child when his father looks him in the eye and deliberately says, "I am well pleased with you." And, there's the quiet joy that arises when your best friend is coming for a visit, and you're preparing a place for him.

The Lord experiences all these feelings at once, along with much more. The Bible calls this the joy of the Lord and it's available to you, not just from time to time, but continually. It's not something you can get by itself, for joy and the Lord are one. Therefore you cannot have full joy without having Him.

A woman named Madame Guyon wrote a book somewhere around 1680. Instead of using the term *abiding in Christ*, she called it *experiencing Christ*. Here are the beginning sentences

---

1. Andrew Murray, *Abide in Christ,* (New Canaan, CT: Keats Publishing, Inc., 1973), p. 127.

of her manuscript. "As you pick up this book, you may feel that you simply are not one of those people capable of a deep experience with Jesus Christ. Most Christians do not feel that *they* have been called to a deep, inward relationship to their Lord. But we have all been called to the depths of Christ just as surely as we have been called to salvation.

"When I speak of this 'deep, inward relationship to Jesus Christ,' what do I mean? Actually, it is very simple. It is only the turning and yielding of your heart to the Lord. It is the expression of love within your heart for him."[1]

In the body of her book, Guyon gave simple steps toward cultivating this relationship with Jesus and then encouraged her readers to throw the steps away the more they become aware of Him. Steps are not the goal—knowing Jesus is. Sadly, many folks love the steps more than Him, and thereby miss the mark.

Her conclusion was this: "All of the Lord's children have been called to the enjoyment of God—an enjoyment that can be known both in *this* life as well as in the life to come. Our state in that day will be one of eternal happiness in union with God. *Our call in this life is the same.*"[2]

It's possible to know God much more deeply than most folks realize. You don't have to be a scholarly sage to do so. You don't even need to know how to read. All you need to know is that your God is good and He wants to draw you into Himself, into a fellowship of joy.

Your role is to believe and let Him draw you. There's no need to plan, scheme, and work your way toward Him. Simply follow His voice. His path often seems to lead in what appears to be the wrong direction. Don't let that bother you; keep following Him. He's the One who knows where to go, and He is a trustworthy guide. The goal isn't perfection, it's not being a good Christian, and it's not happiness. The goal is HIM, the Joy of the whole earth!

---

1. Madame Guyon, *Experiencing the Depths of Jesus Christ* (Goleta, CA: Christian Books, 1981), p. 1.
2. Ibid., p. 135.

The Lord thy God in the midst of thee is mighty;
He will save, He will rejoice over they with joy;
He will rest in His love,
He will joy over thee with singing.
(Zephaniah 3:17)

Questions

- Why did the apostle John write his first letter in the Bible?

- According to Andrew Murray, why do most men never come to the fullness of joy God offers?

- Murray called it *abiding in Christ*. What did Madame Guyon call it?

- Guyon said it was simple to experience Christ. What did she say to do?

Conclusion

Throughout the past year and a half, whenever I've had the opportunity I've walked through the woodshop, entered my office, and climbed into this chair. I've written to you, as personally as possible, how God has expressed Himself to me, especially in the area of happiness. There's much more that could be said; however, for now, it's time to stop.

I've written with the express purpose of seeing men like you enjoying a living relationship with God through the person of Jesus Christ. It's my dream to watch you live responsibly as providers and protectors. I want to see you creating peaceful homes and neighborhoods, giving of your strengths to help those weaker. I want to hear stories of how you've laid aside your selfishness and lived that others might know justice and mercy. I want you to experience the privileges of mature men: the ability to get up after you've fallen and to finish your tasks even though you've turned white with fear.

May God give you courage to be a man. It's for this end that I write.

—*Bob Schultz*
October 2007

P.S. Books are a one-sided conversation. If there's a comment you'd like to make, contact me through the publishers at:

Great Expectations Book Company
PO Box 2067
Eugene, Oregon 97402